Other titles available from the
New Police Bookshop (E Yorks)

TAKING STATEMENTS
Stewart Calligan, seventh edition
ISBN 978-1-903639-23-8 Price £14

THE CUSTODY OFFICER'S COMPANION
Stewart Calligan and Paul Harper, fourth edition
ISBN 978-1-903639-18-4 Price £19.95

POLICING YOUR HEALTH
Stewart Calligan and Alan Charlesworth (editors)
first edition 978-0-9533058-8-9 Price £10

To order the above titles please email
policebooks@aol.com

Prices include postage and packing
Bulk orders (10 copies or more) 10% discount
Cheques should be made payable to the
New Police Bookshop

www.policebooks.org.uk

PREFACE

'HOW TO USE THE LAW FOR PRACTITIONERS'

Simplicity is an aid to learning. With this statement in mind, I have chosen some 70 offences which can be found in the Police Summons and Charges lists and in the Magistrates' Court Sheets on most days of the week across the country.

Less common offences have not been included and this simplification has allowed me to spend more time on the type of offences you are likely to be concerned with.

The main problems encountered by people dealing with the detection, prosecution and the defence of offences are:

(A) What are the POINTS TO PROVE
(B) What do the points MEAN and
(C) How are the points PROVED or DISPROVED.

In some of the offences I have added a further heading of
(D) Supporting Evidence,
where other important matters are explained.

(A) Shows the correctly worded Summons or Charge, called **points to prove**. Each offence has been divided into its different elements, all of which have to be proved beyond all reasonable doubt for a successful prosecution.
(B) and **(C)** headings are drawn from legislation, case decisions and the normal practice of magistrates' courts.

It should be noted that the practice of some police personnel to refer to case decisions as 'stated cases' is wrong. Only those cases stated from magistrates' courts to Crown courts or a High court on a point of law are 'stated cases'. It is safer, therefore, to refer to all as 'case decisions'.

LAYOUT OF THE BOOK

Section 1 deals with **TRAFFIC**
A Glossary is provided for the traffic offences at the beginning of Section 1 of the book.

Section 2 deals with **CRIME**

Section 3 with **MISCELLANEOUS OFFENCES**

Section 4 with **POWERS OF ARREST** and **SEIZURE OF MOTOR VEHICLES.**

NINTH EDITION JULY 2016

This edition includes law and procedure changes, repeals and additions which include new case law, alterations to the parking at night offence, section 5 Public Order Act 1986, Offensive Telephone Calls, Criminal Damage and the Rave offence etc, plus section 141 Criminal Justice Act 1988 which - from 18.08.2016 - includes 'Zombie knives' and bans their sale, manufacture, rental or importation.

ACKNOWLEDGMENTS

I am greatly indebted to Colin Connolly Cert Ed of the Humberside Police Training Department, Superintendent S Hellawell LLB, PC J Manning BA, Susan Turner of the New Police Bookshop, and my wife, Christine, for the production of this book.

Stewart Calligan
Yorkshire, 2016

SUMMARY OF CONTENTS

PREFACE iv

CONTENTS

Offences listed chronologically vii

Section 1 Traffic

Section 2 Crime

Section 3 Miscellaneous

Section 4 Police Powers

Offences listed alphabetically x

Section 1 Traffic Offences

Section 2 Crime

Section 3 Miscellaneous

Section 4 Police Powers

SECTION 1 1

Traffic and Glossary

SECTION 2 105

Crime

SECTION 3 205

Miscellaneous Offences

SECTION 4 241

Powers of the Police

CONTENTS

Offences listed chronologically

SECTION 1 - TRAFFIC

Traffic Glossary Page No

Drive 2
Motor vehicle 3
Mechanically propelled vehicle 4
Road 4
Public place 6
That you 6
Trailer 7
Use, cause or permit 7
Vehicle 8
Questioning 8

Offence Page No

1 Careless and inconsiderate driving (due care) 9
2 Obstruction - unnecessary 14
3 Failing to stop after an accident 17
4 Disqualified driving 21
5 Using etc without insurance 23
6 Using etc without test certificate 28
7 No crash helmet 31
8 No vehicle licence 33
9 Misuse of trade licence/plates 36
10 Windscreen washers not fitted or not working 41
11 Lights in poor visibility conditions 43
12 Fail to comply with constable's/warden' signal 45
13 Driving without a licence 48
14 Failing to display 'L' plates 51
15 Provisional licence holder unaccompanied 54
16 Provisional licence holder carrying passenger on motorcycle 56
17 Driving with excess alcohol 60
18 Failure to wear a seat belt 65
19 Dangerous parts 69
20 Defective brakes 72
21 Defective windscreen wipers 75

22 Defective silencer 77
23 Defective tyres 80
24 Quitting without stopping engine/setting brake 84
25 Horns not fitted 87
26 Pedestrian failing to comply with constable's direction 90
27 Parking on wrong side at night 92
28 Fail to conform to Pelican/Puffin lights 95
29 Defective side lights 97
30 Interference with vehicles 100
31 Mobile phone use while driving 102

SECTION 2 - CRIME

Offence Page No
1 Wasting police time 106
2A Fear or provocation of violence 109
2B Conduct likely to cause harassment/alarm/distress 115
2C Intention to cause harassment/alarm/distress 120
2D Stalking etc without violence 122
2E Racially or religiously aggravated offences 126
Racial/religious aggravation chart....................128
Pointers to building good race relations....................132
3A Indecent exposure....................134
3B Exposure....................135
4 Telephone calls - offensive etc 138
5 Offensive weapon 141
6 Assault occasioning actual bodily harm 144
6A Common assault 145
7 Assault on police 148
8 Obstructing police 150
9 Sexual assault....................151
10 Soliciting for prostitution....................157
10A Soliciting a prostitute....................160
11 Taking conveyance without authority 162
12 Burglary - committing theft having entered 164

13 Theft 167
14 Fraud by false representation 170
15 Handling stolen goods 174
16 Criminal damage 179
17 Trespassing with a firearm 184
18 Going equipped for burglary or theft 186
19 Making off without payment 188
20 Robbery 192
21 Unlawful possession of a controlled drug 194
22 Possession of a controlled drug with intent to supply 197
23 Abstracting electricity 199
24 Passing counterfeit notes and coins 201

SECTION 3 - MISCELLANEOUS OFFENCES

Offence Page No
1 Dogs worrying livestock 206
2 Possessing etc shotgun without a certificate 208
3 Discharging firearm near highway 211
4 Drinking under age 213
5 Found drunk 216
6 Drunk and disorderly 218
7 Litter offence 220
8 Sporting events - control of alcohol....222
9 Trespassing on land 227
10 Ticket tout offence 230
11 Taxi tout offence 233
12 Poaching at night 235
13 Rave offence....237

SECTION 4 - POWERS OF THE POLICE

New powers Page No
1 Arrest 242
2 Seizure of motor vehicle....243

Offences listed alphabetically

SECTION 1 - TRAFFIC

Careless and inconsiderate driving (due care) **1** 9
Dangerous parts **19** 69
Defective brakes **20** 72
Defective side lights **29** 97
Defective silencer **22** 77
Defective tyres **23** 80
Defective windscreen wipers **21** 75
Disqualified driving **4** 21
Driving with excess alcohol **17** 60
Driving without a licence **13** 48
Fail to conform to constable's/warden' signal **12** 45
Fail to conform to Pelican/Puffin lights **28** 95
Fail to display 'L' plates **14** 51
Fail to stop after an accident **3** 17
Fail to wear a seat belt **18** 65
Glossary....2
Horns not fitted **25** 87
Interference with vehicles **30** 100
Lights in poor visibility conditions **11** 43
Misuse of trade licence/plates **9** 36
Mobile phone use while driving **31** 102
No crash helmet **7** 31
No vehicle licence **8** 33
Obstruction - unnecessary **2** 14
Parking on wrong side at night **27** 92
Pedestrian failing to comply with constable's direction **26** 90
Provisional licence holder carrying passenger on motorcycle **16** 56
Provisional licence holder unaccompanied **15** 54
Quitting without stopping engine/setting brake **24** 84
Using etc without insurance **5** 23
Using etc without test certificate **6** 28
Windscreen washers not fitted or not working **10** 41

SECTION 2 - CRIME

Abstracting electricity **23** 199
Assault occasioning actual bodily harm **6** 144
Assault on police **7** 148
Burglary - committing theft having entered **12** 164
Common assault **6A** 145
Conduct likely to cause harassment/alarm/distress **2B** 115
Criminal damage **16** 179
Drugs
 Possession of a controlled drug with intent to supply **22** 197
 Unlawful possession of a controlled drug **21** 194
Exposure **3B** 135
Fear or provocation of violence **2A** 109
Fraud by false representation **14** 170
Going equipped for burglary or theft **18** 186
Handling stolen goods **15** 174
Indecent exposure **3A** 134
Intention to cause harassment/alarm/distress **2C** 120
Macpherson Report advice - building good race relations **2E** ... 132
Making off without payment **19** 188
Mobile phone offences
 Telephone calls - offensive etc **4** 138
 Stalking etc without violence **2D** 122
Obstructing police **8** 150
Offensive weapon **5** 141
Passing counterfeit notes and coins **24** 201
Possession of a controlled drug with intent to supply **22** 197
Racially or religiously aggravated offences **2E** 126
Robbery **20** 192
Sexual assault **9** 151
Soliciting a prostitute **10A** 160
Soliciting for prostitution **10** 157
Stalking etc without violence **2D** 122
Taking conveyance without authority **11** 162

Telephone calls - offensive etc **4**....138
Theft **13**....167
Trespassing with a firearm **17**....184
Unlawful possession of a controlled drug **21**....194
Vehicle taking - Taking conveyance without authority **11**....162
Wasting police time **1**....106

SECTION 3 - MISCELLANEOUS OFFENCES

Alcohol at sporting events **8**....222
Discharging firearm near highway **3**....211
Dogs worrying livestock **1**....206
Drinking under age **4**....213
Drunk and disorderly **6**....218
Found drunk **5**....216
Litter offence **7**....220
Poaching at night **12**....235
Possessing etc shotgun without a certificate **2**....208
Rave offence **13**....237
Sporting events - control of alcohol **8**....222
Taxi tout offence **11**....233
Ticket tout **10**....230
Trespassing on land **9**....227

SECTION 4 - POWERS OF THE POLICE

Arrest **1**....242
Powers of the Polce....242
Seizure of motor vehicle **2**....243

Section 1

Traffic

TRAFFIC GLOSSARY

DRIVE

The 'driver' means the person having control of the direction and movement of the vehicle. Drive and driving are construed accordingly. In most of the authoritative cases the 'direction' is taken to be the steering and the 'movement' is taken to be the acceleration and braking.

Problems arise where a person is not fully in control of direction and movement. In *Ames v MacLeod* 1969 SC 1 and *R v McDonagh* [1974] RTR 372 a test was suggested, namely 'whether the person was in a substantial sense controlling the movement and direction of the car'. However, where this test is satisfied it may still not be conclusive proof that the person is 'driving' and it must be asked whether the person can be said to be 'driving' under the ordinary meaning of the word.

Examples which have been held to be 'driving' which do not readily fall within the above definition include:

(1) Where a girl was in the front passenger seat and leaned across to the driver's side, controlling the steering wheel with both hands, being within reach of the ignition and the hand brake. Her companion in the driver's seat who controlled the gears and the foot controls was also held to be driving.

(2) A person sitting behind the steering wheel being pushed by people outside the vehicle, if s/he is acting in conjunction with those pushing. The people pushing will aid and abet the driver.

(3) A learner driver sitting behind the steering wheel in a dual control vehicle is a driver although the qualified driver also has control of the vehicle and can also be said to be driving. A person supervising a learner driver in a single control vehicle may aid and abet the commission of an offence by the learner driver.

(4) A 'steersman' in a towed vehicle will be held to be 'driving' if the extent and degree of control could be said to correctly describe 'driving' (*R v McDonagh* [1974] RTR 372 and

McQuaid v Anderton [1980] 3 All ER 540).

(5) Pedalling an auto-assisted bicycle without starting the engine has been held to be driving away.

(6) It is felt that a person propelling a motor cycle with legs astride the cycle and feet on the ground by 'paddling' it, would be driving.

(7) 'Wheel spinning' can be driving even if no forward movement takes place (*DPP v Alderton* [2004] RTR23).

MOTOR VEHICLE

A 'motor vehicle' means a mechanically propelled vehicle intended or adapted for use on roads, section 185 (1) Road Traffic Act 1988.

A good illustration of 'intended' is found in the case of *Childs v Coghlan* (1968) 112 SJ 175 where a 30 ton earth mover which was made for use on construction sites and not roads was held to be a motor vehicle. As it was too large to be put on a lorry to be moved from site to site it had to travel on roads under its own power and was held to be intended to be used on roads.

Dumper trucks will normally not be classified as motor vehicles as they are not intended or adapted for use on roads. A go-kart is in a similar position, but both a dumper truck and a go-kart can become 'motor vehicles' if it can be proved that they have been adapted or intended for use on roads.

Use of a vehicle at any particular time does not prove 'intended'. Proof of regular use on the road is usually called for. 'Adapted' means fit and apt for the purpose. A test was laid down in 1987 as to whether a vehicle was intended or adapted for use on roads. It is whether a reasonable person, looking at the vehicle, and forming a view as to its general use, would say the vehicle might well be used on the road (*Chief Constable of Avon and Somerset v Fleming* [1987] 1 All ER 318).

Vehicles which are not to be treated as motor vehicles include pedestrian-controlled mechanically propelled vehicles and electrically assisted pedal cycles, section 189 Road Traffic Act 1988.

MECHANICALLY PROPELLED VEHICLE

As a start one should ask 'Is the vehicle constructed so that it can be mechanically propelled?' ie is there a mechanical means of propulsion, other than 'person power' as in pedalling a bicycle?

Mechanical propulsion presently ranges from steam, through the various petrols and oils to gas and electric.

Helpful explanations can be found in the following cases:

(1) Don't ask whether the engine is in working order but ask, 'Is the vehicle constructed so that it can be mechanically propelled?' *R v Tashin* [1970] RTR 88.

(2) A temporary removal of the engine does not stop a vehicle being a 'mechanically propelled vehicle', *Newberry v Simmonds* [1961] 2 All ER 318.

(3) The opposite to (2) above was held where the vehicle was a broken down wreck in *Smart v Allan* [1962] 3 All ER 893.

(4) But see *Binks v Department* of the Environment [1975] 119 SJ 304 where a severely damaged car which the owner intended to repair, was held to be a mechanically propelled vehicle. *Plumbien v Vines* [1996] Crim LR 124, held that a motor vehicle ceases to be a motor vehicle only where it has decayed (been damaged or dismantled) to such an extent that only extensive restoration would recreate it as a working mechanically propelled vehicle.

(5) 'Go-peds' or motorised scooters have been held to be motor vehicles intended for use on roads (*Chief Constable of North Yorkshire Police v Saddington* [2001] Crim LR 41).

(6) In *DPP v King* [2008] EWHC 447 (Admin) it was held the 'City Mantis' electric scooter was a motor vehicle. The judge applied the objective 'reasonable person' test.

ROAD

Road is defined as any highway and any other road to which the public has access and includes bridges over which a road passes, section 192 Road Traffic Act 1988.

'Highway' is narrower in meaning than road and there must be some evidence of permanent dedication to the public. A court should take any map or plan etc into account when deliberating on the question of what is a highway.

Note. There is a rebuttable presumption that the highway includes everything between the fence or boundary wall etc, eg grass verges, footpaths and central reservations. But this is so only where the fence etc was erected with reference to the highway and would probably not apply where the fence was erected for some other reason (*A-G v Beynon* [1969] 2 All ER 263).

To amount to a 'road', the public must have legal and actual access. It must allow travellers to move from one place to another along a definable route with ascertainable edges. The question of whether a 'road' has been defined in law is a question of fact for the court to decide. The main factor for a road is public access, but where to draw the line causes difficulty. It was held in *Cox v White* [1976] Crim LR 263 that a mere slight degree of access by the public is not sufficient.

General cases of interest concerning this definition include:

(1) *Harrison v Hill* 1932 SC (J) 13 where a road maintained by a farmer, leading from the public road to his farmhouse, was held to be a road. It was also used by people having no business at the farm although from time-to-time the farmer turned away people who were using it.

(2) In *Bugge v Taylor* [1940] 104 JP 467 the forecourt of a hotel was held to be a road. It was private property, but was used as a short cut from one street to another.

Note. For 'road' there must be a line of communication which can be described as a road and it is not sufficient merely to show vehicles have access, eg to a car-park.

(3) In *Cutter v Eagle Star Insurance Company Ltd* [1998] it was held that a car park is not a road in the 'ordinary use of language', as a car park and road have separate characteristics and functions. A road enables movement to particular destinations and a car park enables stationary vehicles to stand and wait.

PUBLIC PLACE

'Public place' has been added to certain offences under the road traffic legislation to enlarge the use of the offences. Although not defined under the Road Traffic Act 1988, having regard to the spirit of the legislation, it is considered that the definitions used in other Acts would apply.

These definitions include any place to which the public have access, whether on payment or otherwise, eg fields where the public can park for a race meeting or traction engine rally, footpaths or bridleways (unless the Act states otherwise: see section 22A (5) of the Road Traffic Act 1988), or anywhere where the public could lawfully be at risk from mechanically propelled vehicles.

It has been held that a 'public place' includes a multi-story car park when there was no barrier restricting entrance. *Bowman v DPP* [1991] RTR 263.

Conversely it has been held that the following were not public places - a public house car park outside licensing hours, or land open only to members of a proprietary club.

THAT YOU

'That you' prefaces most summons headings and merely means that the prosecution must be in a position to prove that the defendant in court is the person whom they allege committed the offence. It is very unlikely, although not unknown, that the defendant will deny being present etc, at the time of the offence.

The defendant may still plead not guilty while admitting that s/he is the person concerned in the alleged offence.

When identity is in question, consider *R v Turnbull and Others* [1976] 3 All ER 549. Courts will normally look for the following points in disputed identity cases.

The eight points of *Turnbull:*

(1) How long did the witness observe the accused?
(2) How far away from the witness was the accused person?
(3) What were the lighting conditions at the time?
(4) Was the observation impeded in any way?

(5) Had the witness ever seen the accused before; if so, how often?
(6) If the witness had only seen the accused occasionally, had the witness any special reason for remembering the accused?
(7) How long was the period of time between original observation and subsequent identification to the police?
(8) Was there any material discrepancy between the description of the accused given to the police by the witness when first seen and his/her actual appearance?

It is important that these points be addressed during the collection of evidence.

TRAILER

Trailer means vehicle drawn by a motor vehicle, section 185 Road Traffic Act 1988.

'Vehicle' was discussed in *Boxer v Snelling* [1972] RTR 472 where it was said that, in borderline cases, not only the construction or nature of the contrivance but also the circumstances of its use should be taken into account. A stall with wheels was held to be a vehicle in this case.

A motor vehicle which is being towed by another motor vehicle both remains a motor vehicle and also becomes a trailer. Therefore, such a towed motor vehicle can be subject to offences of using without tax or insurance or in contravention of the Construction and Use Regulations.

USE, CAUSE OR PERMIT

'Use' means 'to have the use of the motor vehicle on a road'. The following cases will help to illustrate the variety of uses recognised by the courts:

(1) a vehicle placed on a road with the battery removed and incapable of being driven at all;
(2) when stationary on a road for loading or unloading;
(3) a vehicle being towed is apparently being 'used'.

Note. Where the offence in question gives alternatives of using, causing or permitting the use thereof, 'uses' is interpreted rather more strictly and restrictively than when an offence commences 'Did use', with no other alternatives. In such a restricted case, where there is a master-servant relationship it can usually be said that the master or employer 'uses' as well as the driver, being the servant or employee.

In *Green v Burnett* [1954] 3 All ER 273 it was held that an employer was guilty of 'using', as a vehicle with defective brakes was being used on his business. The Motor Vehicle (Construction and Use) Regulations generally impose an absolute liability even though an employer, as in this case, had no knowledge of the defect. In effect there is no necessity for *mens rea* or guilty knowledge in using offences.

In practice, 'use' is probably the easiest to prove and the hardest to disprove.

'Cause' means some express or positive mandate from the person 'causing' to the driver etc. *Mens rea* or guilty knowledge must be proved by the prosecution where a person is reported for an offence of 'causing'.

'Permit' means an express or implied permission and does not involve any order to take a vehicle on the roads. As with 'cause' *mens rea* must be proved.

VEHICLE

This is wider in meaning than 'motor vehicle' as 'vehicles' do not need to be mechanically propelled. Therefore, trailers and bicycles, as well as all kinds of mechanically propelled vehicles, are 'vehicles'. A court will most likely look at the circumstances in which the article was used, as well as the construction, nature or function of it, in cases of difficulty.

QUESTIONING

When asking questions at the roadside, eg dealing with traffic offences, the suspect should, if not under arrest, be:

(a) cautioned; and
(b) told s/he is not under arrest and is free to leave.

OFFENCES

1. CARELESS AND INCONSIDERATE DRIVING

Section 3 Road Traffic Act 1988 as amended by the Road Traffic Act 1991

(A) POINTS TO PROVE

1. That you 2. did drive 3. a certain mechanically propelled vehicle, namely a .... 4. on a road or other public place called .... 5. (a) without due care and attention or (b) without reasonable consideration for other persons using the road or public place.

(B) MEANING OF TERMS

- **1. 'That you'** Means the person driving the mechanically propelled vehicle (ie identity).
- **2. 'did drive'** See Glossary.
- **3. 'a certain mechanically propelled vehicle, namely a ...'**

This phrase replaces 'motor vehicle' as defined in the Glossary. In the case of certain motor vehicles such as dumper trucks, the prosecution had to prove that they were intended or adapted for use on roads. All this offence now requires is that the vehicle in question is mechanically propelled, see Glossary.

- **4. 'on a road or other public place called ....'**

See Glossary for 'road'. The phrase 'other public place' has been added. Although not defined it is considered that the definition used in other Acts will apply ie, 'Includes any place to which the public have access, whether on payment or otherwise'. Suffice it to say that the offence can now be committed in many more places than before, see Glossary.

- **5. (a) 'without due care and attention'** Means that if (and only if) the way the driver drives falls below what would be expected of a competent and careful driver, s3ZA(2). In deciding 'what would be expected' regard shall be given to the circumstances of which the driver could be expected to be aware and also to any circumstances shown to have been within the knowledge of the accused, s3ZA(3). Things 'expected' would include the speed limit, weather conditions etc; things shown to have been 'known' could include that s/he knew it was an accident black spot, s/he knew oil had been spilt on the road, s/he was tired.

■ **5. (b) 'without reasonable consideration for other persons using the road'.**

Means his/her driving 'inconvenienced the other persons', s3ZA(4). Examples could include driving too slowly, not dipping headlights and splashing pedestrians from puddles on the road.

Dangerous driving is usually reserved for intentional dangerous driving or where it can be proved the defendant was driving in such a way as to fall within the definition of 'driving dangerously' in the Road Traffic Act 1988.

(C) USUAL METHODS OF PROVING THESE POINTS

■ **1. 'That you'** Cases are sometimes lost when the prosecution fails to identify the driver. This can be done simply by a witness being asked in court, 'Is the defendant the man you saw driving at the time of the offence?'

Problem areas include where two people share the controlling of the movement and direction of the vehicle. It was held in *Tyler v Whatmore* [1976] RTR 83 that two people can actually drive the same vehicle, at the same time. Here the front seat passenger leaned across the person sitting in the driver's seat and with both hands on the steering wheel, steered the car. The other person still controlled the propulsion.

Another problem arises where two people admit to being the driver of a vehicle and the police are unable to prove or disprove either statement. Offences such as wasting police time, obstructing police and perverting the course of justice could be considered, with the possibility of both being taken to court as drivers and letting the court decide.

■ **2. 'did drive'** Driving is usually proved by witness statements to the effect that they saw the defendant drive. In the absence of witnesses, only a confession on the part of the defendant or sufficient circumstantial evidence will substantiate the offence. Circumstantial evidence may include that the defendant was the only person with the car keys; s/he was seen getting out of the vehicle; s/he was seen going towards or getting in the vehicle and/or s/he said s/he was going to drive the vehicle.

■ **3. 'a certain mechanically propelled vehicle, namely a ....'** 'Mechanically propelled vehicle' can be proved by a phrase in a witness statement to the effect, 'I saw him/her driving a Jaguar saloon motor car, registered number ....'

In borderline cases, such as broken down vehicles or power assisted pedal cycles, recourse must be had to the case law. See Glossary. No doubt more case law will be forthcoming on the meaning of 'mechanically propelled'. For 'go-peds' see traffic glossary under 'mechanically propelled vehicles'.

Expert evidence from a suitably qualified mechanical engineer may be necessary on a few occasions.

■ **4. 'on a road or other public place called ....'**

'Road' is defined as 'any highway or any other road to which the public has access and includes bridges over which a road passes'. In problematical cases the following test might help: 'Does the general public have access?'

If 'Yes', then it is a road. If 'No', then is a majority class or a minority class restricted from using it? If only a minority class, then it will probably still be a road but if otherwise, generally not, unless it is a 'public place' (see Glossary).

Where a road is shown on a 'definitive' map prepared under the Countryside Act 1968, Schedule 3, as a 'byway open to all traffic' this can be taken as conclusive evidence that the public has access.

However, where a right of way was only shown as a footpath on a definitive map, the court can still hold that it was a 'road', *Attorney General v Honeywill and Others* [1972] 3 All ER 641.

■ 5(a) 'without due care and attention'

'Due care and attention' can be proved by witnesses stating that they saw the defendant 'drive round the roundabout and wander into the side of another car' or 'brake rather late and run into the car in front' or by the defendant stating that 'I misjudged the gap or distance' or 'I didn't see the other car, motorbike, cycle or pedestrian, etc'. These are all examples of driving that 'falls below that of a competent and careful driver.

'What the accused should have known' and 'what s/he did know' can also be proved. Questions such as 'Were you aware of the stop sign?' or 'Did you feel tired before you veered off the road?' would help prove what s/he should have known/did know.

■ 5(b) 'without reasonable consideration for other persons using the road'.

This can be proved by a statement from a witness who saw the actions which amounted to the inconvenience of the other persons. The defendant may wish to make a statement under caution which may prove or help to prove these elements.

(D) SUPPORTING EVIDENCE

Generally the following excuses etc are pertinent to this offence:

(a) Automatism: Any involuntary movement of body or limb, eg epileptic fit, or under attack from a swarm of bees. This is usually a good defence and should be borne in mind when preparing the case.

(b) The offender's non-observance of other vehicles or traffic signs etc is generally no defence, eg 'I didn't see the other car' or 'I didn't see the "stop" sign'.

(c) Excuses based on weather conditions, visibility and the condition of the road surface etc are generally poor defences, unless the driver takes immediate evasive action. Where a driver says 'I was blinded by the sun' or 'There was a patch of fog' or 'The road was covered with black ice', s/he should have stopped, reduced his/her speed or driven at a speed which was safe. If s/he drove on regardless of the conditions s/he could well be convicted.

When compiling a case, attention must be paid to the prevailing conditions, especially where relevant excuses are put forward, eg in a case where the effect of weather may be a possible defence.

(d) Mechanical defect: The defence of any mechanical defect that caused or contributed towards the offence is normally good. But where the defect or fault should have been detected during normal maintenance, this would not constitute a defence and there would probably be an offence under the appropriate Construction and Use Regulations. In the case of *R v Spurge* [1961] 2 All ER 688 it was held that it was at least careless driving where the driver took a vehicle on a road, knowing there was a defect such as defective steering or brakes.

(e) Defences based on matters outside the driver's control, such as a dog running into the path of the car or a tree being blown across the road are generally good. The presence of the dog at the time of the offence is hard to disprove in the absence of the dead or injured dog, or a witness.

(f) The Highway Code does not create offences but can be quoted by the prosecution or defence to help negate or establish liability.

(g) Evidence of speed at the time of the offence can be established from the length of skid marks, the severity of any impact damage or from witnesses etc.

(h) Other minor points which may be helpful would include: the position of the gear lever after an accident; what the speedometer registers if damaged in an accident; the position of other instruments, such as obligatory light switches or windscreen wiper switches; whether the driver had consumed any alcohol prior to the offence (provided the prejudicial value does not outweigh the evidential value of such evidence) and the mechanical condition of the vehicle.

(i) Sudden illness or losing consciousness would normally avail the driver of a defence unless losing consciousness was as a result of the driver's actions such as a deliberate overdose or taking illegal substances.

Note 1. A notice of intended prosecution is required for this offence if no accident has occurred. In *Gidden v CC Humberside* [2009] EWHC 2924 (Admin) it was held that an NIP sent by first class post was not properly served as it was delivered two days after the 14 day limit due to a postal strike. In such cases it is for the authorities to use other means of warning the accused.

Note 2. The two offences created by section 3, ie 'due care' or 'reasonable consideration' should not be charged as alternatives. One or the other should be chosen based on the evidence available.

2. OBSTRUCTION

Regulation 103 Road Vehicle (Construction and Use) Regulations 1986, and s42 Road Traffic Act 1988

(A) POINTS TO PROVE

1. That you 2. being the person in charge
3. of a certain motor vehicle (or trailer) namely a ....
4. did cause (or permit) that motor vehicle (or trailer)
5. to stand on a road called ....
6. so as to cause an unnecessary obstruction thereof.

(B) MEANING OF TERMS

■ **1. 'That you'** Means the identity of the person in charge.

■ **2. 'being the person in charge'**

Means that such a person generally has the keys for the vehicle, but in the vast majority of cases the person 'in charge' will be the driver who parks the vehicle resulting in the obstruction.

■ **3. 'of a certain motor vehicle (or trailer) namely a ....'**

See Glossary for 'motor vehicle' and 'trailer'.

■ 4. did cause (or permit) that motor vehicle or trailer'

See Glossary.

■ 5. 'to stand on a road called ....'

Generally 'to stand' means to allow the motor vehicle (or trailer) to remain stationary and does not necessarily mean unattended (*Hinde v Evans* (1906) 70 JP 548) although this will normally be the case.

■ 6. 'so as to cause an unnecessary obstruction thereof'.

The judges have taken the word 'unnecessary' to mean 'unreasonable', whether or not use amounting to an obstruction was or was not unreasonable use is a question of fact, depending on all the circumstances, including:

(i) the length of time the obstruction continued;
(ii) the place where it occurred;
(iii) the purpose for which it was done;
(iv) whether it caused an actual as opposed to a potential obstruction as quoted in *Evans v Barker* [1971] RTR 453. Commonplace obstructions include restricting the width of the road, blocking footpaths if they form part of the road and obstructing pedestrians and vehicles at 'T' junctions and other types of junctions etc.

Note the Middlesex Crown Court case of *Langham v Crisp* [1975] Crim LR 652 where a motorist parked on one side of the road and an obstruction was caused by the subsequent parking of cars opposite. It was held that when the first vehicle parked it was not done 'so as to cause' an unnecessary obstruction.

(C) USUAL METHODS OF PROVING THESE POINTS

■ 1. 'That you'

See (C)1 of Offence 1.

■ 2. 'being the person in charge'

This point is usually proved by asking the person suspected of parking or causing the vehicle to be parked in the offending position, 'Are you responsible for this vehicle being left in this position?'

■ 3. 'of a certain motor vehicle (or trailer) namely a ....'

See Glossary, and for trailer a witnesses description of the trailer and coupling would suffice.

■ 4. 'did cause (or permit) that motor vehicle (or trailer)'

See (C)2 of offence 5, although it is felt that 'permit' in this offence means the continuing obstruction while 'cause' deals with the positioning of the vehicle on the road. (See [1975] Crim LR 653.)

■ 5. 'to stand on a road called ....'

'To stand' can be proved by the police officer who observed the vehicle stationary on a road. For 'road' see (C)4 of Offence 1.

■ 6. 'so as to cause an unnecessary obstruction thereof'.

This point can best be proved by a police officer who observes some actual unnecessary obstruction of the road causing other road users inconvenience, delay, or complete blockage of the road etc. Such evidence is given by phrases including, 'I saw women with prams obstructed by the offending vehicle parking across a pavement'; 'several motor cars had to negotiate carefully and slowly to pass the offending vehicle' etc. A sketch plan may assist the court where the obstruction is difficult to describe in words.

(D) SUPPORTING EVIDENCE

Note 1. A fixed penalty ticket could be issued for this offence.

Note 2. Also be aware of the offence of leaving a vehicle on a road in a potentially dangerous position contrary to section 22 Road Traffic Act 1988. Examples to show the difference between this offence and unnecessary obstruction include leaving a vehicle around a blind bend, or just over a humpback bridge. A notice of intended prosecution is required for this offence.

Note 3. Also be aware of the offence of wilfully obstructing the free passage of a highway with anything - not just a vehicle - contrary to the Highways Act 1980, section 137.

Note 4. See Removal and Disposal of Vehicle Regulations 1986.

3. FAILING TO STOP AFTER AN ACCIDENT

Section 170 Road Traffic Act 1988

(A) POINTS TO PROVE

1. That you 2. being the driver 3. of a certain mechanically propelled vehicle, namely .... 4. owing to the presence of which 5. on a road or other public place called .... 6. an accident occurred whereby injury was caused to another person (or damage was caused to another vehicle or to an animal or to property) 7. did fail to stop.

(B) MEANING OF TERMS

■ 1. 'That you'

Means the person driving the mechanically propelled vehicle, ie, his/her identity.

■ 2. 'being the driver'

'Driver' means the person who takes the mechanically propelled vehicle on the road. The driver continues to be 'the driver' until the journey is finished, although s/he may have stopped and switched the engine off some minutes before (*Jones v Prothero* [1952] 1 All ER 434.) A person who has parked his/her car on a road and left it unattended can't be said to be the driver for the purposes of this offence.

■ 3. 'of a certain mechanically propelled vehicle namely ....'

See (B)3 of Offence 1.

■ 4. 'owing to the presence of which'

This point means that there must be a direct connection between the mechanically propelled vehicle and the occurrence of the accident: *Quelch v Phipps* [1955] 2 All ER 302. Therefore a passenger jumping off a moving bus and injuring him/herself would bring the motor vehicle within this section, but not generally where a driver has left his/her stationary motor vehicle parked on a road. See *Cawthorn v DPP* [2000] RTR 45 where it was held that the driver was still 'the driver' when leaving the vehicle to post a letter, the vehicle rolled downhill and hit a wall.

■ 5. 'on a road or other public place called ....'

See (B)4 of Offence 1.

■ 6. 'an accident occurred whereby injury was caused to another person (or damage was caused to another vehicle or to an animal or to property)'

'Accident' means an unintended occurrence which has an adverse physical result (*R v Morris* [1972] 1 All ER 384). It can also include an accident resulting from a deliberate act (*Chief Constable of West Midlands Police v Billingham* [1979] Crim LR 256). No other vehicle need be involved as where a person or animal or property is involved (*R v Pico* [1971] Crim LR 599).

'Injury' includes shock, or a hysterical and nervous condition (*R v Miller* [1954] 2 All ER 529 and *Bourhill v Young* [1943] AC 92.

'Another person' means other than the driver, therefore where only the driver is injured this section is not applicable.

'To another vehicle' means that damage must be caused to a vehicle other than the driver's motor vehicle. Therefore where only the driver's motor vehicle is damaged the section does not apply. Note that this phrase applies to 'another vehicle' and not 'another motor vehicle'. 'Vehicle' has been held to include a bicycle (*Ellis v Nott-Bower* [1896] 60 JP 760).

'Animal' means horse, cattle, ass, mule, sheep, pig goat or dog. Notable exceptions are cats and poultry, but criminal damage could be considered. In *Mutton v Bates* [1983] 147JP459 it was held the driver need not go and search for other parties.

'Property' means property growing in, constructed on, fixed to, or forming part of, the land adjacent to the road or on the road itself. Therefore trees, crops, lamp post, traffic signs, walls etc will generally be included in section 170.

■ 7. 'did fail to stop'.
Means did fail to stop immediately the accident happened and remain at the scene of the accident long enough, taking the prevailing conditions into account, to give his/her name and address and also the name and address of the owner and the identification marks of the vehicle (*Lee v Knapp* [1966] 3 All ER 961 and *Ward v Rawson* [1979] Crim LR 58). The obligation to stop arises almost immediately the accident happens. The driver should stop almost immediately, as soon as it is convenient and safe to do so (*Hallinan v DPP* [1998] Crim LR754). Two separate offences are created by section 170, namely (1) failing to stop and (2) failing to give particulars (*Roper v Sullivan* [1978] Crim LR 233).

If a motor vehicle is stationary when the accident occurs the driver must remain at the scene until s/he has satisfied the section. But note that s/he need not wait indefinitely (*Norling v Woolacott* [1964] SASR 377). If particulars are not given at the scene, then they must be reported at a police station as soon as reasonable practicable and in any case within 24 hours.

(C) USUAL METHODS OF PROVING THESE POINTS

■ 1. 'That you' See (C)1 of Offence 1.

■ 2. 'being the driver' This point will be proved by a witness seeing the defendant driving away etc. Where there are no witnesses or they cannot be traced, an admission by the defendant either verbally to the officer dealing with the case (who would record the admission in his/her pocket book or accident booklet) or in writing if s/he chooses to make a 'voluntary' statement in accordance with the Codes of Practice.

Also see (C)2 of Offence 1.

■ 3. 'of certain mechanically propelled vehicle, namely ......'
See (C)3 of Offence 1.

■ 4. 'owing to the presence of which'
This point is normally covered in any witness statement that

might be available, viz, 'I saw four vehicles were involved etc' or 'if it had not been for that vehicle the accident would not have happened'. Where witnesses are unavailable an admission to being involved is helpful.

■ 5. 'on a road or other public place called ....'

See (C)4 of Offence 1.

■ 6. 'an accident occurred whereby injury was caused to another person (or damage was caused to another vehicle or to an animal or to property)'

This point is normally proved by the police officer examining the vehicles concerned or person, animal or property involved and recording the details of damage or injury in his/her pocket book or accident booklet. Where a person is injured it is normal practice to take a statement to the effect that 'the following injuries were sustained'. In some cases of damage it might be wise to ascertain whether or not there was any similar damage prior to the accident. In this way a defence that the property was already damaged and that the defendant is not responsible for the present damage can be countered.

■ 7. 'did fail to stop'.

It is rare for a police officer to witness such an event, therefore in most cases the evidence of passers-by or the driver of the other vehicle involved will have to be relied upon.

Obviously, the best kind of evidence in such cases is the evidence of 'independent' witnesses, ie a witness not concerned with the parties involved in the accident. Where the only evidence available is that of one party against the other, or a wife giving evidence for her husband, or an employee giving evidence for the employer etc the court may well find the case not proved.

A good practical point to include is a statement that there was an interested party at the scene, had the defendant stopped. In other words, an injured pedestrian or the driver of a damaged vehicle had remained at the scene. Had the defendant stopped s/he could have given his/her particulars to such a person.

(D) SUPPORTING EVIDENCE

This offence was absolute, ie no *mens rea* was required. However in *Harding v Price* [1948] 1 All ER 283 it was held that if the driver did not know he had been involved in an accident the section did not apply. Therefore in borderline cases the prosecution might have to rely on evidence of the severity of injury and damage, or the noise of the accident, to help prove to the court beyond all reasonable doubt that the driver must have realised that s/he had been involved in an accident.

An example of when a driver may not be aware of an accident would be if a large articulated motor vehicle, when turning a sharp corner, had a slight collision with a parked car. If the police could not prove that the accident was of such force and severity that the driver must have known of the accident, then the defence could put forward the saving in *Harding v Price.*

Note. As section 170 creates two offences, if the defendant fails to stop but later reports the accident, or stops but refuses to give any particulars, an offence is committed as per *North v Gerish* (1959) 123 JP 313.

4. DISQUALIFIED DRIVING

Section 103(1)(b) Road Traffic Act 1988

(A) POINTS TO PROVE

1. That you 2. being disqualified for holding or obtaining a licence to drive a motor vehicle (if of a certain class, state) 3. drove a certain motor vehicle, namely a .... (if of a certain class, state) 4. on a road called ....

(B) MEANING OF TERMS

■ 1. 'That you'

Means the person driving the motor vehicle, ie identify the driver.

■ 2. 'being disqualified for holding or obtaining a licence to drive a motor vehicle'

Disqualification means that the person disqualified must not, in Great Britain, drive on a road any motor vehicle. As a last resort the solicitor present at the disqualification could be called as a witness (*R (Howe) v South Durham Magistrates' Court* 168JP424. NB: The defendant could admit the disqualification under caution.

■ 3. 'did drive a certain motor vehicle, namely a ....'

See Glossary.

■ 4. 'on a road called ....'. See Glossary.

(C) USUAL METHODS OF PROVING THESE POINTS

■ 1. 'That you'

See (C)1 of Offence 1; also *R v Turnbull and Others* in the Glossary under, 'That you'.

■ 2. 'being disqualified for holding or obtaining a licence to drive a motor vehicle'

Proof of disqualification may be certificate of conviction or extract from the magistrates' court's register together with proof of identification of the defendant, eg by the police officer who was present in court when the defendant was disqualified. An admission that s/he was disqualified will suffice (*Moran v CPS* [2000] 164 JP 562). This procedure varies according to local practice and enquiries regarding the best method of proof are advised.

■ 3. did drive a certain motor vehicle, namely a ....'

See (C)2 of Offence 1 for 'drive' and Glossary for 'motor vehicle'.

■ 4. 'on a road called ....'.

See (C)4 of Offence 1.

(D) SUPPORTING EVIDENCE

Problems related to the identity of the driver occur quite frequently with this offence. A police officer may see a person driving a motor vehicle, whom s/he knows to be disqualified, but is not in a position to stop the driver. When eventually interviewed regarding the suspected offence there may be a denial and, while not essential, the prosecution case would be stronger if corroboration is available regarding the driver's identity. (See the eight points of *R v Turnbull and Others* in the Glossary, under 'That you'.)

Note 1. Where a defendant states that s/he did not know that he was disqualified this will not amount to a defence, *Taylor v Kenyon* [1952] 2 All ER 726.

Note 2. An under-age driver should be prosecuted for not having the appropriate driving licence, not for the above offence.

5. USING ETC WITHOUT INSURANCE

Section 143 Road Traffic Act 1988

(A) POINTS TO PROVE

1. That you 2. did use (or cause, or permit .... to use) 3. a motor vehicle, namely a .... 4. on a road or other public place called .... 5. there not being in force in relation to the use of that vehicle 6. such a policy of insurance or security 7. in respect of third party risks as complies with the requirements of Part VI, Road Traffic Act 1988.

(B) MEANING OF TERMS

■ 1. 'That you'

Means the person using, causing or permitting the use of the motor vehicle ie identify the offender.

■ 2. 'did use (or cause, or permit .... to use)'

See Glossary.

■ 3. 'a motor vehicle, namely a ....' See Glossary.

■ 4. 'on a road or other public place called ....'

See Glossary.

■ 5. 'there not being in force in relation to the use of that vehicle'

This phrase means that there is no insurance cover in force relating to the use of the vehicle as opposed to insurance covering the contents for example.

■ 6. 'such a policy of insurance or security'

A policy is of no effect until the certificate is delivered to the assured (section 147(1) Road Traffic Act 1988). The policy is the contractual document setting out the terms and conditions of the insurance agreement which appear in various paragraphs which are usually called clauses.

■ 7. 'in respect of third party risks as complies with the requirements of Part VI Road Traffic Act 1988'.

Section 145 Road Traffic Act 1988 sets out the requirements for third part risks as follows.

'(2) The policy must be issued by an authorised insurer.

'(3) Subject to subsection (4) below, the policy:

(a) must insure such person, persons or classes of persons as may be specified in the policy in respect of any liability which may be incurred by him/her or them in respect of the death of or bodily injury to any person caused by, or arising out of, the use of the vehicle on a road in Great Britain and,

(aa) must, in the case of a vehicle normally based in the territory of another member state, insure him/her or them in respect of any civil liability which may be incurred by him/her or them as a result of an event related to the use of the vehicle in Great Britain (GB);

(b) must in the case of a vehicle normally based in GB, insure him/her/them in respect of any liability which may be incurred by him/her/them in respect of the use of the vehicle, and of any trailer, whether or not coupled - in the territory other than GB and Gibraltar of each of the member states of the Communities according to the law on compulsory insurance against civil liability in respect of the use of

vehicles of the state where the liability may be incurred; and
(c) must also insure him/her or them in respect of any liability which may be incurred by him/her or them under the provisions of this Part of this Act relating to payment for emergency treatment.

'(4) The policy shall not by virtue of subsection (3)(a) above, be required to cover:
(a) liability in respect of the death, arising out of and in the course of his/her employment, of a person in the employment of a person insured by the policy or of bodily injury sustained by such a person arising out of and in the course of his/her employment; or, [other such matters. (See section for full list.)]'

(C) USUAL METHODS OF PROVING THESE POINTS

■ **1. 'That you'** See (C)1 of Offence 1.

■ **2. 'did use (or cause, or permit .... to use)'**

'Use' is generally proved by the observation of the police officer to the effect, 'I stopped the motor vehicle .... which was being driven in Queens Street and spoke to the driver ....'

A few offences of this nature will involve the owner of the vehicle or employer of the driver. For example the owner of a motor vehicle can be said to use it where s/he sits at the side of the driver, who is not his/her employee and the vehicle is being used for his/her purpose (*Cobb v Williams* [1973] RTR 113).

An employer 'uses' the vehicle, even when not present in it, when it is being used on his/her business, with his/her permission. Therefore, where the driver is accompanied by the owner, or the motor vehicle is being used on firm's business, the driver and the owner or employer all 'use'.

Where the owner is present in the vehicle, the police officer's statement will include an admission as to the vehicle's ownership eg, 'Are you the owner of this vehicle?' and the passenger replies, 'Yes'.

In cases involving an employer, s/he will probably have to be interviewed later. Questions such as, 'Are you the company secretary or owner of .... firm?'; 'Is your firm the owner of motor vehicle ....?' and 'Was it being used on firm's business at .... (time) .... in .... (place) .... ?', need affirmative answers. The employer can then be cautioned and reported for the 'using' offence.

Note that a person does not use a vehicle without insurance unless there is an element of controlling, managing and operating the vehicle.

'Cause' can be proved by questions and answers or by instructions written on a job-sheet etc.

Knowledge of the facts amounting to the unlawful use must be shown in the statement of evidence. The driver may provide information that his/her boss said words to the effect that s/he knew there was no insurance but the vehicle was the only one available and the journey had to be undertaken.

It has been held that towing a vehicle is 'causing' it to be used (*Milstead v Sexton* [1964] Crim LR 474).

'Permit' is not as precise a term as 'cause' and denotes an express or inferred permission of a general or particular type. Again the prosecution must rely on what the driver tells them or on written instructions and, in rare cases, on admissions by the employer.

'Use' is to be preferred as a charge on the grounds that it is easier to prove, being a clearly defined term, and attracts fewer defences than 'cause' and 'permits'.

■ 3. 'a motor vehicle, namely a ....' See Glossary

■ 4. 'on a road or other public place called ....'

See (C)4 of Offence 1.

■ 5. 'there not being in force in relation to the use of that vehicle'

The proof of insurance falls to the defence once it has been established by the prosecution that the motor vehicle has been used on a road (*Philcox v Carberry* [1960] Crim LR 563).

While the onus is on the defence, most police officers' statements contain the question: 'Are you insured to drive this motor vehicle?' In the cases where an expired insurance certificate is produced a question such as, 'have you any other insurance for this motor vehicle?' is advisable.

■ 6. 'such a policy of insurance or security'

The prosecution must show that the insurance, if any is produced, does not conform to the requirements of section 143 Road Traffic Act 1988, as section 147(1) of that Act requires that for a policy to be effective, the insurers must deliver a certificate in the prescribed form to the assured. The courts recognise the insurance certificate as evidence of being insured. Therefore the police generally require to see the certificate to satisfy themselves that the motor vehicle is correctly insured but in some cases of doubt the policy may have to be examined or inquiries made of the issuing firm.

Evidence of insufficient cover might include someone other than the insured person driving the vehicle; the vehicle being used for the purpose other than agreed, eg for business purposes; or the present vehicle not being entered on the firm's records (this latter being difficult to detect in these days of not generally showing a registered number on a certificate).

■ 7. 'in respect of third party risks as complies with the requirements of Part VI, Road Traffic Act 1988'.

The police officer will normally accept the information on the insurance certificate at face value and if the certificate shows 'comprehensive' cover, this automatically includes 'third party risks'. In a large number of cases the cover will be restricted to 'third party' only which is still within the requirements of section 145 above, at point (B)7 of this offence.

(D) SUPPORTING EVIDENCE

Note 1. When a certificate of insurance has expired or when a new insurance contract is being negotiated, insurance companies issue 'cover notes' which usually vary in length of validity from 15 days to 60 days.

Note 2. For a cover note to be valid the defendant must accept the cover note and rely upon it for his/her insurance cover. If s/he disregards it because s/he intends to insure with another firm, for example, and never pays the original firm, the cover note will not be valid *(Taylor v Allon [1965] 1 All ER 557).*

Note 3. As with numerous other offences dealing with road traffic, the use of a motor vehicle without insurance is an absolute offence, ie no guilty knowledge is required.

Note 4. Occasionally when an employee is found to be driving while uninsured on his/her employer's business, the employee can put forward a defence showing:

(a) the vehicle did not belong to him/her; and
(b) was not in his/her possession under a contract of hire or loan;
(c) and, that s/he neither knew nor had reason to believe s/he was driving without insurance.

The employer could still commit the offence of using, causing or permitting no insurance.

Note 5: See power to seize motor vehicles under 'Powers' at the end of the book.

6. USING ETC WITHOUT A TEST CERTIFICATE

Section 47 (1) Road Traffic Act 1988

(A) POINTS TO PROVE

1. That you 2. did use (or cause, or permit to be used) 3. on a road called .... 4. a motor vehicle, namely a .... (specify type of motor vehicle) to which section 47 of the Road Traffic Act 1988, applied and 5. in respect of which no test certificate had been issued within 12 months prior to the .... day of .... year ....

(B) MEANING OF TERMS

■ 1. 'That you'

Means the person using or permitting the use of the motor vehicle, ie identify the driver etc.

■ 2. 'did use (or cause, or permit to be used)' See Glossary.

■ 3. 'on a road called ....' See Glossary.

■ 4. 'a motor vehicle, namely a .... to which section 47 of the Road Traffic Act 1988 applied and' See Glossary.

Section 47 applies to all motor vehicles first used more than three years before the time at which they are proved to have been actually used on the road for the purpose of the present offence.

The Motor Vehicles (Tests) Regulations 1981 exempt, among other motor vehicles, goods vehicles of an unladen weight exceeding 3,500kg; an agricultural motor vehicle; articulated vehicles; when submitting a vehicle for a test after prior arrangement or bringing it away; where a test certificate is refused - taking it for repair by prior arrangement or bringing it away and also taking it, by towing, to be broken up and motor traders when repairing motor vehicles etc.

■ 5. 'in respect of which no test certificate had been issued within 12 months prior to the .... day of ....'.

This phrase means there was no current test certificate in force for the motor vehicle. A test certificate is valid for 12 months. Some motor vehicles such as taxis need testing every six months.

(C) USUAL METHODS OF PROVING THESE POINTS

■ 1. 'That you'

See (C)1 of Offence 1.

■ 2. 'did use (or cause, or permit to be used)'

See Glossary, also C2 of Offence 5.

■ 3. 'on a road called ......

See Glossary, also C4 of Offence 1.

■ 4. 'a motor vehicle, namely a .... to which section 47 of the Road Traffic Act 1988, applied and' See Glossary.

Proof that the motor vehicle required a test certificate is often overlooked. The majority of this kind of offence will be concerned with motor cars, but whenever the vehicle is of an unusual type the exemptions to the requirements must be carefully checked. Once it has been established that the vehicle or its use is not exempt from the requirement, the type of motor vehicle should be described in the statement. The second requirement is that the date of first registration is more than three years from the date of the suspected offence. Normally this point is proved by the officer in the case examining the registration document and including in his/her statement a passage such as, 'On examining the vehicle's registration document I saw the date of first registration was ....'. If the registration document is lost, or at the DVLA, Swansea, then proof can be requested from DVLA.

■ 5. 'in respect of which no test certificate had been issued within 12 months prior to the .... day of ....'

As with other documents which can be obtained from a number of different places, the onus to show the vehicle had a current test certificate rests on the defendant. An expired certificate might be produced. The particulars should be entered in the officer's pocket book, followed by a question such as, 'Have you any other test certificate for this motor vehicle?' The driver might admit s/he hasn't a current certificate and the relevant conversation can be reproduced in the officer's statement of evidence.

(D) SUPPORTING EVIDENCE

If a police officer has to request a driver to produce a current test certificate, the officer must bear in mind the problem of proving the date of first registration. If a form HO/RT 1 is issued and the driver elects to produce the document at a distant police station it is good practice also to request the suspected driver to produce his/her registration document at the same time. In this way the officer accepting the production can also prove the date of first registration, if need be by personal appearance.

7. NO CRASH HELMET

Regulation 4 Motor Cycles (Protective Helmets) Regulations 1998 and section 16 of the Road Traffic Act 1988

(A) POINTS TO PROVE

1. That you 2. did drive (or ride on) 3. a certain motor bicycle, namely a .... 4. on a road called .... 5. without protective headgear.

(B) MEANING OF TERMS

■ 1. 'That you'

Means the person driving or riding on the motor bicycle, ie the identity.

■ 2. 'did drive (or ride on)'

Refer to Glossary for 'drive'. 'Or ride on' includes any pillion passenger, but not passengers in any sidecar.

■ 3. 'a certain motor bicycle, namely a ....'

Means a two wheeled motor cycle, whether having a sidecar attached thereto or not, and for the purposes of this definition any wheels of a motorcycle shall, if the distance between the centres of the areas of contact between such wheels and the road surface is less than 460 millimetres, be counted as one wheel; per regulation 4(3) of the Regulations.

A mowing machine coming within the definition of a motor bicycle is exempt.

The offence does not include propelling the motor bicycle by a person on foot.

■ 4. 'on a road called ....'

See Glossary.

■ 5. 'without protective headgear'.

'Without' could mean either no headgear at all or a headgear which is not 'protective headgear' as defined: 'protective headgear' means headgear which:

(a) is either -
   (i) a helmet bearing a marking applied by the manufacturer indicating compliance with the specification contained in one of the British Standards mentioned in Schedule 2 (whether or not as modified by any amendment), or
   (ii) a helmet of a type manufactured for use by persons on motor cycles which by virtue of its shape, material and construction could reasonably be expected to afford to persons on motor bicycles a degree of protection from injury in the event of an accident similar to or greater than that provided by the helmet of a type complying with one of the specifications referred to in regulation 5; and

(b) if worn with a chin cup attached to or held in position by a strap or other fastening provided on the helmet, is provided with an additional strap or other fastening (to be fastened under the wearer's jaw) for securing the helmet firmly to the head of the wearer; and

(c) is securely fastened to the head of the wearer by means of the straps or other fastening provided on the headgear for that purpose.

(C) USUAL METHODS OF PROVING THESE POINTS

■ 1. 'That you'

Can be proved as (C)1 of Offence 1.

■ 2. 'did drive (or ride on)'

See (C)2 of Offence 1 for 'drive'. 'Ride on' can be proved by the police officer or witness who saw the offence.

■ 3. 'a certain motor bicycle, namely a ....'

In the vast majority of cases the offender(s) will be on a solo motor bicycle, and occasionally one having a sidecar attached. This fact can be mentioned in the police officer's statement of evidence if s/he witnessed the offence.

■ 4. 'on a road called ....'

See (C)4 of Offence 1; also Glossary.

■ **5. 'without protective headgear'.**

This point can be proved by the police officer's observations that the person on the motor bicycle had no headgear or the headgear s/he was wearing did not come within the legal requirements.

Where it is suspected that headgear is below the British Standard the assistance of a Forensic Science Laboratory could be sought. If the securing straps are not within the legal requirements a full description will be necessary.

(D) SUPPORTING EVIDENCE

Note 1. The Regulations provide the following exemption. 'A requirement imposed by regulations shall not apply to any follower of the Sikh religion while he is wearing a turban.'

Note 2. A crash helmet is required even on a 'roofed' motor cycle (*DPP v Parker* [2004] EWHC 1248).

8. NO VEHICLE LICENCE

Section 29(1) and (3) Vehicle Excise & Registration Act 1994 and section 44 Magistrates' Courts Act 1980

(A) POINTS TO PROVE

1. That you 2. did use (or keep) 3. a mechanically propelled vehicle, namely a .... 4. on a public road called .... 5. for which a vehicle licence was not in force.

(B) MEANING OF TERMS

■ **1. 'That you'**

Means the person using/keeping the motor vehicle, ie their identity.

■ **2. 'did use (or keep)'**

A person 'keeps' a vehicle if s/he causes it to be stationary on a road when not in use. The shortness of the period of time it is left on the road is immaterial (*Holliday v Henry* [1974] RTR 101).

■ 3. 'a mechanically propelled vehicle, namely a ....'

Means propelled by petrol, oil, steam or electricity etc. A vehicle ceases to be mechanically propelled when there is no reasonable prospect of it ever being mobile again (*Binks v Department of the Environment* [1975] RTR 318). Also see Glossary. Certain vehicles are exempt from duty under various Acts. Exemptions likely to be encountered include vehicles not exceeding 10cwt unladen specially adapted for invalids; vehicles brought from abroad for a temporary stay are exempt for a period not exceeding one year from date of importation; vehicles going to or returning from a vehicle test or being repaired etc as a result of the test, provided in all cases prior arrangements have been made. Lists of exemptions can be found in Schedule 2 of the Act.

■ 4. 'on a public road called ....'

'Public road' means 'a road which is repairable at the public expense', per section 62.

■ 5. 'for which a vehicle licence was not in force'.

This phrase means that there was no current vehicle licence in force and this point can be verified by making inquiries at the DVLA, Swansea. A licence is void from the time it was granted where the payment was by a cheque which was eventually dishonoured (Customs and Excise Management Act).

(C) USUAL METHODS OF PROVING THESE POINTS

■ 1. 'That you'

See (C)1 of Offence 1.

■ 2. 'did use (or keep)'

'Use' is usually proved by the police officer in the case giving evidence that s/he saw the defendant driving the motor vehicle in question. Traffic wardens can also become involved with this offence by detecting a vehicle not displaying a current vehicle licence. Where subsequent inquiries show the vehicle to be unlicensed, the traffic warden would be able to prove use.

Similarly, where a vehicle is seen stationary and unattended, the offence of **'keeping'** can be considered. The officer who saw the vehicle being kept should be in a position to state the length of time s/he observed the vehicle being kept on a public road, but see point (B)2 of this offence regarding the length of time kept being immaterial.

Proof of ownership is not required to establish who 'used' or 'kept' the vehicle, but it is advisable that the prosecution should know the owner of the vehicle. An employer is liable for the offence of 'using' an unlicensed vehicle if the vehicle is driven on his/her business and it is no defence for the employer to show that s/he had not authorised the journey if, in fact, the journey was on his/her business (*Richardson v Baker* [1976] RTR 56). The burden of proof regarding the purpose for which the vehicle was used lies on the defence, section 53.

■ 3. 'a mechanically propelled vehicle, namely a ....'

This point is proved by describing the vehicle concerned and making sure it does not come within the many exemptions. 'Mechanically propelled vehicle' does not mean the same as 'motor vehicle' as defined in the Glossary. For the purposes of the Vehicles Excise and Registration Act the vehicle need not be intended or adapted for use on a road. In cases of difficulty the test as mentioned at (B)3 of this offence, ie will the vehicle ever be mobile again, might help in cases where parts have been taken off a vehicle.

■ 4. 'on a public road called ....'

No offence against section 29 is committed where the vehicle is used or kept on a private road, ie a road which is not repairable at public expense. The highways department of the local authority will be able to prove which roads are repairable at public expense where necessary.

■ 5. 'for which a vehicle licence was not in force'.

This point can be proved by an admission on the part of the defendant; on inquiries at the DVLA, Swansea whose records can be produced in evidence; and by an admission on the part of the owner where s/he isn't the defendant etc.

(D) SUPPORTING EVIDENCE

Note. It has been said in the case of *Carpenter v Campbell* [1953] 1 All ER 280 that it may be an oppressive course to prosecute the driver of an unlicensed vehicle in a master-servant relationship, where the driver is the employee and not responsible for licensing the vehicle.

9. MISUSE OF A TRADE LICENCE (OR TRADE PLATES)

Regulation 38 Road Vehicles (Registration and Licensing) Regulations 2002 and sections 11, 12 and 34 Vehicle Excise and Registration Act 1994

(A) POINTS TO PROVE

1. That you, being the holder of a trade licence (or licences) issued under section 11 Vehicle Excise and Registration Act 1994, 2. used by virtue of that (or those) licence (or licences) 3. on a public road called .... 4. a vehicle, namely a .... 5. for a purpose other than a purpose prescribed under section 12 Vehicle Excise and Registration Act 1994 .... specify purpose).

(B) MEANING OF TERMS

■ **1. 'That you, being the holder of a trade licence issued under section 11 Vehicle Excise and Registration Act 1994'**

This means that the defendant must be the person to whom the trade licence was issued. In a large number of cases the licence is issued to a firm, ie a limited company, then the company secretary is liable for the misuse of the trade plate on behalf of the company. The holder of the licence must be a motor trader, vehicle tester or vehicle manufacturer. His/her identity must be proved.

■ **2. 'used by virtue of that licence'**

In other words the vehicle concerned must have been used under the trade licence and not under a normal vehicle excise licence for an offence to contravene the law relating to trade licences.

■ **3. 'on a public road called ....'** See (B)4 of Offence 8.

■ **4. 'a vehicle, namely a ....'**

See (B)3 of Offence 8 for vehicles concerned.

■ **5. 'for the purpose other than a purpose prescribed under section 12 Vehicle Excise and Registration Act 1994'**

Namely in the Road Vehicles (Registration and Licensing) Regulations 1971, regulation 35:

(1) In this regulation, 'business purpose', in relation to a motor trader means:
 (a) a purpose connected with his/her business as a manufacturer or repairer of or dealer in mechanically propelled vehicles; or
 (b) a purpose connected with his/her business as a manufacturer or repairer of or dealer in trailers carried on in conjunction with his/her business as a motor trader, and
 (c) a purpose connected with his/her business of modifying vehicles prior to the first registration... or of valeting vehicles.

(2) For the purposes of sub-paragraphs (a) to (k) of paragraph (4) of this regulation, where a mechanically propelled vehicle is used on a public road by virtue of a trade licence and that vehicle is drawing a trailer, the vehicle and trailer shall be deemed to constitute a single vehicle.

(3) Save as provided in regulation 36 of these regulations, no person, being a motor trader and the holder of a trade vehicle, shall use any mechanically propelled vehicle on a public road by virtue of that licence unless it is a vehicle which is temporarily in his/her possession in the course of his/her business as a motor trader or a recovery vehicle kept by

him/her for the purpose of dealing with disabled vehicles in the course of that business.

(4) Save as provided in the said regulation 36 and without derogation from the provisions of the last preceding paragraph of this regulation, no person, being a motor trader and the holder of a trade licence, shall use any mechanically propelled vehicle on a public road by virtue of that licence for a purpose other than a business purpose and other than one of the following purposes:

(a) for its test or trial or the test or trial of its accessories or equipment in the ordinary course of construction, modification or repair or after completion in either such case;

(b) for proceeding to or from a public weighbridge for ascertaining its unladen weight or to or from any place for its registration or inspection by a person acting on behalf of the Secretary of State;

(c) for its test or trial for the benefit of a prospective purchaser, for proceeding at the instance of a prospective purchaser to any place for the purpose of such test or trial, or for returning after such test or trial;

(d) for its test or trial for the benefit of a person interested in promoting publicity in regard to it, for proceeding at the instance of such a person to any place for the purpose of such test or trial, or for returning after such test or trial;

(e) for delivering it to the place where the purchaser intends to keep it;

(f) for demonstrating its operation or the operation of its accessories or equipment when being handed over to the purchaser;

(g) for delivering it from one part of his/her premises to another part of his/her premises, or for delivering it from his/her premises to the premises of, or between parts of premises of, another manufacturer or repairer of or dealer in mechanically propelled vehicles or removing it from the premises of another manufacturer or repairer of or dealer in mechanically propelled vehicles direct to his/her own premises;

(h) for proceeding to or returning from a workshop in which a body or a special type of equipment or accessory is to be or has been fitted to it or in which it is to be or has been painted, valeted or repaired;

(i) for proceeding from the premises of a manufacturer or repairer of or dealer in mechanically propelled vehicles to a place from which it is to be transported by train, ship or aircraft or for proceeding to the premises of such a manufacturer, repairer or dealer from a place to which it has been so transported;

(j) for proceeding to or returning from any garage, auction room or other place at which vehicles are usually stored or usually or periodically offered for sale and at which the vehicle is to be or has been stored or is to be or has been offered for sale as the case may be;

(k) for proceeding to or returning from a place where it is to be or has been tested, or for proceeding to a place where it is to be broken up or otherwise dismantled.

(C) USUAL METHODS OF PROVING THESE POINTS

■ 1. 'that you, being the holder of a trade licence issued under section 11 Vehicle Excise and Registration Act 1994'

Has a slightly different meaning than the offence where the driver is required to be identified. In this case the prosecution must prove that the person who has been summonsed is the holder of the trade licence. In some cases s/he will be the driver of the vehicle. It can be proved that s/he was the holder by examining the trade licence itself for the defendant's name, by an admission from the defendant and by checking with the issuing authority.

■ 2. 'used by virtue of that licence'

This point can be proved by asking the trade licence holder 'was (or is) this vehicle being used under this trade licence?' If the vehicle is driven by an employee who is not to be summonsed for any offence, a statement should be requested as s/he should be dealt with as a witness. S/he should be asked to mention in his/her statement the fact that the vehicle was being used by virtue of the trade licence.

■ 3. 'on a public road called ....'

See the comments made at Offence 8(C)4, ie the road must be repairable at public expense.

■ 4. 'a vehicle, namely a ....'

As excise duty is the subject matter of this offence the same vehicles that are exempt from vehicle excise licences are also exempt from the necessity for a trade licence, therefore refer to offence 8(C)3 for more information.

■ 5. 'for a purpose other than a purpose prescribed under section 12 Vehicle Excise and Registration Act 1994'.

The purpose is proved by question and answer if the defendant is driving or if s/he has to be interviewed later by a police officer. A statement from any employee who could help prove this point would be valuable for the prosecution, especially if it is suspected the defence will deny the alleged purpose. The garage foreman who perhaps sent the employee driver on the journey could be asked to provide a statement. Illegal uses often include shopping trips, collecting spare parts for the garage or calling at a public house along a journey. Each use will present its own problems of proof and it is impossible to lay down any hard and fast rules.

(D) SUPPORTING EVIDENCE

Where the prosecution allege a contravention of the trade plate law there will probably be the further offence of 'no vehicle licence', see Offence 8.

10. WINDSCREEN WASHERS NOT FITTED OR NOT WORKING

Regulation 34(2) Road Vehicles (Construction and Use) Regulations 1986 and section 42 Road Traffic Act 1988

(A) POINTS TO PROVE

1. That you 2. did use (or cause, or permit to be used) 3. on the road called .... 4. a motor vehicle namely a .... 5. which was required to be fitted with windscreen wipers 6. which was not fitted with windscreen washers capable of cleaning in conjunction with those wipers the area of windscreen swept by the wipers.

(B) MEANING OF TERMS

■ 1. 'That you'

Means the user's etc identity.

■ 2. 'did use (or cause, or permit to be used)'

See Glossary.

■ 3. 'on a road called ....'

See Glossary.

■ 4. 'a motor vehicle namely a ....'

See Glossary.

■ 5. 'which was required to be fitted with windscreen wipers'

This point means that regulation 34(1) of the above regulations requires every vehicle which is fitted with a windscreen to be fitted with one or more wipers.

One exception to this requirement is in circumstances in which a view to the front can be obtained without first looking through the windscreen, for example, by opening or looking over it.

■ 6. 'which was not fitted with windscreen washers capable of cleaning in conjunction with those wipers the area of windscreen swept by the wipers'.

This point means that where a motor vehicle is required to be fitted with wipers it must also have washers. The washers must be correctly aligned, filled with fluid and be otherwise correctly maintained, so as to be capable of cleaning in conjunction with the wipers.

(C) USUAL METHODS OF PROVING THESE POINTS

■ 1. 'That you'

See (C)1 of Offence 1.

■ 2. 'did use (or cause, or permit to be used)'

See (C)2 of Offences 5 and 19.

■ 3. 'on a road called ....'

See (C)4 of Offence 1.

■ 4. 'a motor vehicle namely a ....'

See Glossary

■ 5. 'which was required to be fitted with windscreen wipers'

This point is proved by showing there was no view to the front without first looking through the windscreen. This point is usually included in the police officer's statement of evidence, eg, 'The driver could not get a view to the front without first looking through the windscreen'.

■ 6. 'which was not fitted with windscreen washers capable of cleaning in conjunction with those wipers the area of windscreen swept by the wipers'.

This point can be proved by showing in the police officer's evidence the actual situation regarding washers, ie whether any washers were fitted; if fitted, whether there was any fluid in the reservoir; or whether the jets were correctly adjusted etc. The main point to show is that the washers were not capable of cleaning as required.

11. LIGHTS IN POOR VISIBILITY CONDITIONS

Regulation 24 Road Vehicles Lighting Regulations 1989 and section 42(1) Road Traffic Act 1988

(A) POINTS TO PROVE

1. That you 2. did use 3. a vehicle namely a .... 4. which carried obligatory lamps 5. on a road called ...... 6. between the hours of sunrise and sunset without the lamps being lit while the vehicle was in motion 7. during a period of seriously reduced visibility on that road.

(B) MEANING OF TERMS

■ 1. 'That you'

Means the identity of the person using the vehicle.

■ 2. 'did use'

See Glossary. Cause and permit may be committed.

■ 3. 'a vehicle namely a ....'

The term is wider than motor vehicle and has been held to include a bicycle

■ 4. 'which carries obligatory lamps'

'Obligatory lamps', in relation to a vehicle, means such of the obligatory front lamps, obligatory headlamps and obligatory rear lamps as the vehicle is required, by virtue of the Road Vehicles Lighting Regulations, to carry when on a road during the hours of darkness (as defined by the Road Vehicles Lighting Regulations).

■ 5. 'on a road called'

See Glossary.

■ 6. 'between the hours of sunrise and sunset without the lamps being lit while the vehicle was in motion'

'Without the lamps being lit' is self-explanatory. It is thought that this means all must be working to comply with this regulation. 'While the vehicle was in motion' means that the vehicle must be moving either backwards or forwards and that these regulations do not apply when the vehicle is stationary.

■ 7. 'during a period of seriously reduced visibility conditions on that road'.

'Seriously reduced visibility conditions' in relation to a vehicle used on a road between the hours of sunrise and sunset (ie daytime) may include such conditions adversely affecting visibility (whether consisting of, or including, fog, smoke, heavy rain or spray, snow, dense cloud, or any similar condition) as seriously reduce the ability of the driver (after the appropriate use by him/her of any windscreen wiper and washer) to see other vehicles or persons on the road, or the ability of other users of the road to see the vehicle.

(C) USUAL METHODS OF PROVING THESE POINTS

■ 1. 'That you'

See (C)1 of Offence 1.

■ 2. 'did use'

See (C)2 of Offence 5.

■ 3. 'a vehicle namely a ....'

'Vehicle' is proved by describing it in a prosecution witness' statement.

■ 4. 'which carried obligatory lamps'

Can be proved by describing which obligatory lamps it carried in a witness' statement.

■ 5. 'on a road called ....'

See (C)4 of Offence 1.

■ 6. 'between the hours of sunrise and sunset without the lamps being lit while the vehicle was in motion'

'The hours of sunrise and sunset' can be proved by reference to an almanac or from a witness' observations if this is found necessary. The lamps not being lit and the motion of the vehicle can be proved by the observations of a prosecution witness, ie usually the constable who reports the offender for summons, eg, 'The vehicle's obligatory lights were not lit and the vehicle was in motion on the road'.

■ 7. 'during a period of seriously reduced visibility conditions on that road'.

Can be proved by describing the conditions according to the definition at (B)7 of this offence. This is a question of fact for the court to decide, and so it is essential for the prosecution to show that the conditions seriously reduced the driver's ability to see other vehicles etc. The offending driver may occasionally admit this fact, but failing this, poor visibility must be proved.

(D) SUPPORTING EVIDENCE

Note 1. Where a headlamp is capable of emitting a dipped beam and a full or main beam, then either beam would be sufficient. A matched pair of front fog lamps can be substituted for headlamps in conditions of fog or falling snow.
Note 2. Section 24(1)(a) as above covers 'in motion' and section 24(1)(b) covers 'at rest', ie parked or stationary.

12. FAIL TO COMPLY WITH CONSTABLE'S OR WARDEN'S SIGNAL

Section 35(1) Road Traffic Act 1988

(A) POINTS TO PROVE

1. That you 2. being the person driving (or propelling) 3. a vehicle, namely a .... 4. where a police constable (or a traffic warden) was for the time being engaged in the regulation of traffic 5. on a road called ....
6. did neglect (or refuse) to stop the vehicle (or to make the vehicle proceed in a particular line of traffic or to make the vehicle keep to a particular line of traffic or to proceed to a particular point)
7. when directed so to do by the police constable (or the traffic warden) in the execution of his/her duty.

(B) MEANING OF TERMS

■ 1. 'That you'

The identity of the person driving or propelling the vehicle.

■ 2. 'being the person driving (or propelling)'

'Propelling' means that vehicles other than mechanically propelled are included, such as pedal cycles.

■ 3. 'a vehicle, namely a ....' See Glossary.

■ 4. 'where a police constable (or a traffic warden) was for the time being engaged in the regulation of traffic'

This offence cannot be committed where the constable or traffic warden is not engaged in the regulation of traffic. This duty is derived from the constable's common law duty to act in protection of life and property. Therefore, refusing to proceed to a census point (or a traffic survey being carried out on or in the vicinity of a road) is an offence under this section. A designated Community Support Officer (CSO) has the same power as a Police Constable under this section.

■ 5. 'on a road called ....' See Glossary.

■ 6. 'did neglect (or refuse) to stop the vehicle (or to make the vehicle proceed in a particular line of traffic or to make the vehicle keep to a particular line of traffic or to proceed to a particular point)'

This phrase means:

(a) 'neglect to stop' caters for cases where the driver does not see the constable's signal. It appears from the case decisions on this point that if the court feels that the driver should have seen the signal then the offence will be committed;

(b) 'refuse to stop' is straightforward refusal when such conduct can be proved;

(c) 'stop' apparently means to stop and remain stationary until signalled to move;

(d) 'proceed in a particular line of traffic' means eg to signal the driver etc, to join a line of traffic;

(e) 'keep to a particular line' means, for example, to continue in the line in which s/he is already travelling;

(f) 'proceed to a particular point' means eg to signal the driver to go from A to B or start a particular line of traffic etc.

In *Kaba v Dpp* [2014] (Unreported Queen's Bench Division) it was held that 'causing an obstruction' or 'failing to comply with a traffic direction' is committed even though the obstruction was only 30 to 40 seconds.

■ 7. 'when directed to do so by the police constable (or the traffic warden) in the execution of his/her duty'

The constable or warden should be acting with a view to protecting life or property as in point 4 of this offence. The direction or signal by the officer should be given clearly and in sufficient time for the defendant to stop. It has been held that a signal which was given with a lamp at night and which the driver failed to understand was not sufficient for proving failing to stop.

(C) USUAL METHOD OF PROVING THESE POINTS

■ 1. 'That you'

See (C)1 of Offence 1.

■ 2. 'being the person driving (or propelling)'

See (C)2 of Offence 1.

■ 3. 'a vehicle, namely a ....'

Vehicle is proved by describing it in a witness' statement.

■ 4. 'where a police constable (or a traffic warden) was for the time being engaged in the regulation of traffic'

This point is proved by stating so in the constable's or warden's statement of evidence, eg, 'I was engaged in the regulation of traffic to allow pedestrians to cross safely'.

■ 5. 'on a road called ....'

See (C)4 of Offence 1.

■ 6. 'did neglect (or refuse) to stop the vehicle (or to make the vehicle proceed in a particular line of traffic or to make the vehicle keep to a particular line of traffic or to proceed to a particular point)'

The proving of this phrase will depend on the circumstances of each case. If there is an obvious refusal to stop the vehicle the officer should show this in his/her statement. The fact that the driver did not stop can be explained or whichever part of this point is applicable. If more than one officer or warden witnessed the incident it might save argument in court if a corroborative statement was made by the other witness.

■ 7. 'when directed so to do by the police constable or the traffic warden) in the execution of his/her duty'.

This first point 'when directed to do so' is proved by the officer or warden describing how visible s/he was to the driver, for example: 'I was clearly visible to a driver approaching the cross-roads etc... Visibility was good, the weather was fine and the sun was not shining etc...' The police officer or warden should then describe his/her signal in detail.

'The execution of his/her duty' is proved as at point 4 above.

(D) SUPPORTING EVIDENCE

Note 1. The vehicle need not be on a road at the time of the offence. The section only requires that the constable or warden should be on a road and a driver entering a road from a private drive in contravention of a constable's signal under this section could commit an offence.

Note 2. Under this section the constable need not be in uniform in comparison with section 163 of the Road Traffic Act 1988 which deals with the general power to stop vehicles. See end of book for Power of Arrest.

Note 3. A notice of intended prosecution is required.

Note 4 A Fixed penalty may be issued.

13. DRIVING WITHOUT A LICENCE

Section 87 Road Traffic Act 1988

(A) POINTS TO PROVE

1. That you 2. did drive 3. a motor vehicle, namely a .... 4. on a road called .... 5. otherwise than in accordance with a licence 6. authorising you to drive a vehicle of that class.

(B) MEANING OF TERMS

■ 1. 'That you'

Means the person driving the motor vehicle, ie his/her identity.

■ 2. 'did drive' See Glossary.

■ 3. 'a motor vehicle, namely a ....' See Glossary.

■ 4. 'on a road called ....' See Glossary.

■ 5. 'otherwise than in accordance with a licence'

Means a domestic driving licence, British forces licence, Northern Ireland Licence, and exchangeable licence from certain non EC countries or community licences etc.

■ 6. 'authorising you to drive a vehicle of that class'

'Class' of vehicle shall be construed as reference to a class defined or described by reference to any characteristics of the vehicles or to any other circumstances whatsoever (section 192(3) Road Traffic Act 1988).

These different 'classes' include motor bicycle; motor tricycle; motor car; goods vehicles; motor vehicles having over eight but under 17 seats (in addition to the driver); agricultural tractors and mopeds.

(C) USUAL METHODS OF PROVING POINTS

■ 1. 'That you' See (C)1 of Offence 1.

■ 2. 'did drive' See (C)2 of Offence 1.

■ 3. 'a motor vehicle namely a ....'

See Glossary

■ 4. 'on a road called ....'

See (C)4 of Offence 1.

■ 5. 'otherwise than in accordance with a licence'

In most cases the suspected driver will either say s/he has no licence or s/he will elect to produce a licence and fail to do so.

Therefore, questions put to the defendant such as, 'Have you ever passed a Ministry of Transport test for this class of vehicle?' and/or, 'Do you hold or have you ever held a driving licence for this class of vehicle?' should prove useful.

■ 6. 'authorising you to drive a vehicle of that class'

Nine times out of 10 the vehicle concerned will be a motor bike or a motor car. But it is important to be able to classify the different types of mechanically propelled vehicles in order to be able to prove to a court in which class a vehicle falls.

(D) SUPPORTING EVIDENCE

It will assist the court if the reason for not having a licence can be mentioned in evidence. This can be done by putting a suitable question to the defendant and recording his/her reply.

This is an absolute offence (ie not requiring any guilty knowledge or *mens rea*). It may be committed by those over the age of 70 (whose licences are renewable every three years), provisional licence holders on expiry of such a licence, and people suffering from certain disabilities who can only hold licences for restricted periods.

In a few cases the defendant will have deliberately driven without a licence. The reasons may be because s/he cannot pass a test; is too young; is a visitor to Britain, or is a new resident who has been here for more than 12 months and can no longer drive on his/her foreign licence (and therefore has to pass a British driving test). Such knowledge on the part of the defendant should be proved to the court as the sentence will usually be heavier.

Note 1. It could be unlawful to act as a steersman without a driving licence, see Glossary.

Note 2. Statutory exemptions are provided in section 88 of the Road Traffic Act 1988 and, *inter alia*, allow a person to drive without a licence or cause or permit another to do so if the driver has held or is entitled to obtain a licence for that class of vehicle and an application for such a licence has been

received including in it the date s/he was driving.
Note 3: See Section 4 'Powers of the Police' at the end of the book for possible seizure of the motor vehicles.
Note 4. The onus of proving that s/he has a licence is on the driver.

14. FAILING TO DISPLAY 'L' PLATES

Regulation 16 Motor Vehicles (Driving Licences) Regulations 1999

(A) POINTS TO PROVE

1. That you 2. being a person to whom a provisional licence to drive a motor vehicle had been granted 3. failed to comply with a condition subject to which it was granted in that 4. you drove (or rode) 5. on a road called .... 6. a motor vehicle, namely a .... 7. without there being displayed in such a manner as to be clearly visible to other persons using the road from within a reasonable distance from the front and back of the vehicle 8. 'L' plates (or 'D' plates in Wales) in the prescribed form.

(B) MEANING OF TERMS

■ **1. 'That you'**

Means the person driving the motor vehicle, ie identify the driver.

■ **2. 'being a person to whom a provisional licence to drive a motor vehicle had been granted'**

Means that the defendant must be issued with a current provisional licence for the class of vehicle s/he was driving or riding.

■ **3. 'failed to comply with the conditions subject to which it was granted'**

Means that one of the conditions of the provisional licence has not been complied with, ie failing to display 'L' plates in this case (or 'D' plates in Wales).

■ **4. 'you drove (or rode)'** See Glossary.

■ **5. 'on a road called ....'** See Glossary.

■ **6. 'a motor vehicle, namely a ....'** See Glossary.

■ **7. 'without being displayed in such a manner as to be clearly visible to other persons using the road from within a reasonable distance from the front and back of the vehicle'**

This element means that the 'L' plate must be unobscured by articles, dirt, snow etc, kept straight, and not wrapped around the forks of the motor bike or the bumper bar of a car etc.

■ **8. 'L plates in the prescribed form (D plates in Wales)'.**

The prescribed form states that the plates should be a white 178mm (7in) square with a red letter 'L' thereon, 102mm (4in) high, 89mm (3.5in) wide and 40mm (1.5in) thick (with similar specification for the optional 'D' plate in Wales). Note that though the 'D' plate may be displayed in Wales, this should be replaced with an 'L' on driving into England.

(C) USUAL METHODS OF PROVING THESE POINTS

■ **1. 'That you'** See (C)1 of Offence 1.

■ **2. 'being a person to whom a provisional licence to drive a motor vehicle had been granted'**

This is usually proved by the police officer in the case examining the current provisional licence. S/he can simply state in evidence that s/he examined the licence and found it to be a current provisional. The details of the licence must be recorded in the pocket book and are usually required in a statement.

A question to the effect, 'Have you any other licence for this vehicle or have you ever passed a Department of Transport test for this vehicle?' can be put to the defendant and entered in the officer's statement of evidence together with the negative reply. Should the reply be in the affirmative then the offence would not be committed.

■ **3. 'failed to comply with a condition subject to which it was granted'**

This element is proved by outlining the fact that 'L' plates were not displayed as required by law.

■ 4. 'you drove (or rode)'

See (C)2 of Offence 1.

■ 5. 'on a road called ....'

See (C)4 of Offence 1.

■ 6. 'a motor vehicle, namely a ....'

See Glossary.

■ 7. 'without there being displayed in such a manner as to be clearly visible to other persons using the road from within a reasonable distance from the front and back of the vehicle'

The police officer's evidence is required to the effect that 'L' plates were not displayed in such a manner as to be clearly visible. For example, both 'L' plates were missing, one of the two was missing, that the white surround had been cut off, that the 'L' plates were torn, dirty or otherwise illegible. Mitigation can be provided for the defendant if evidence is given that bits of string or sticky tape showed where 'L' plates had been fitted.

■ 8. 'L plates in the prescribed form'.

Proof is required that the size, shape or colour were not as prescribed or that there were no 'L' plates or only one displayed. Note that the Welsh alternative to the 'L' plates, the 'D' plate, is permitted in Wales.

(D) SUPPORTING EVIDENCE

Note. Generally the offence is straightforward as outlined, but if an unlicensed pillion passenger on a motor bicycle persuaded the rider to take off his/her 'L' plates, or the passenger took them off himself, s/he would aid and abet the rider's offence of no 'L' plates. The motive behind this action is usually to reduce the chances of a police check of two on a motor bicycle. Such checks are frequent where there are two on a motor bicycle with 'L' plates.

15. PROVISIONAL LICENCE HOLDER UNACCOMPANIED

Regulation 16 Motor Vehicles (Driving Licences) Regulations 1999

(A) POINTS TO PROVE

1. - 6. (as offence 14) 7. being a class or description which s/he was authorised to drive by virtue of the provisional licence; 8. otherwise than under the supervision; 9. of a qualified driver; 10. who was present with him/her in or on the vehicle.

(B) MEANING OF TERMS

■ 1. - 6.

As Offence 14.

■ 7. 'being a class or description which s/he was authorised to drive by virtue of a provisional licence'.

As Offence 14.

The class or description of the motor vehicle when the provisional licence holder is required to be accompanied is as shown in his/her provisional licence.

■ 8. 'otherwise than under the supervision'

It is a question of fact in each case whether or not the qualified driver was supervising. The duty of the supervisor is to prevent the learner from acting unskillfully or carelessly or in a manner likely to cause danger to others. If the 'qualified driver' does not do what can be reasonably expected of him/her regarding these duties the learner could be said to be not under supervision.

■ 9. 'of a qualified driver'

The supervisor must be a 'qualified driver' as defined by regulation 17 of the Motor Vehicles (Driving Licences) Regulations 1999, namely, a person who holds a full licence authorising him/her to drive as a full licence holder a motor vehicle of the same class or description as the vehicle being driven by the holder of the provisional licence; who is at least 21 years of age and who has held a full licence for at least three years.

■ **10. 'who was present with him/her in or on the vehicle'.**
The learner cannot argue that s/he was being correctly supervised by someone standing on the footpath or in radio contact with him/her etc, the supervisor must be in or on the vehicle at all times.

(C) USUAL METHOD OF PROVING THESE POINTS

■ **1. to 6.** as Offence 14.

■ **7. 'being a class or description which s/he was authorised to drive by virtue of a provisional licence'**
By showing in the police officer's statement of evidence that the provisional licence s/he held covered the class of vehicle s/he was driving. If not authorised to drive the class in question the correct offence would be driving without a licence (Offence 13).

■ **8. 'otherwise than under the supervision'**
The most usual way of proving this point will be that the learner was alone in the vehicle. Occasionally s/he will be accompanied by a 'qualified driver' but because such person was asleep, drunk or poorly etc, the learner would not be classed as being supervised. The observations of a witness or an admission by the accused would prove this point.

■ **9. 'of a qualified driver'**
This point is proved by examining the details of the licence of anyone accompanying the learner to see if the licence complies with the definition of qualified driver at (B)9 of this offence. If it does there is no offence. A police officer can demand the production of the driving licence of a 'qualified driver' under the Road Traffic Act.

■ **10. 'who was present with him/her or on the vehicle'.**
This is proved as at (C)8 of this Offence, inasmuch as the learner will be alone in the vehicle.

(D) SUPPORTING EVIDENCE

Note 1. A supervisor can aid and abet the learner to drive while over the prescribed limit etc. A conviction ensued where the supervisor had been drinking with the driver who was seen to swerve from side to side (*Crampton v Fish* (1969) 113 SJ 1003).
Note 2. Grandfather rights, ie those who passed their test before 1 January 1997, no longer permitted to supervise learner driver unless passed relevant test for that category of vehicle (Reg 17 as amended).

16. PROVISIONAL LICENCE HOLDER CARRYING PASSENGER ON A MOTORCYCLE

Regulation 16(6) Motor Vehicles (Driving Licences) Regulations 1999

(A) POINTS TO PROVE

1. to 5. (as offence 14); 6. a motor vehicle, namely .... 7. while carrying on it another person.

(B) MEANING OF TERMS

■ **1. to 5.** As Offence 14

The officer dealing must have a basic knowledge of the complex law which now applies to obtaining a driving licence for a motor cycle. This is as follows:

The rider must complete compulsory basic training (CBT)] before riding a moped or motorcycle (with or without sidecar) on the road. However, s/he or she may ride on a road under the supervision of an approved instructor as part of that training course. From 1st January 1997 all learner moped and motorcycle riders, irrespective of when a licence was issued, must have completed a Compulsory Basic Training (CBT) course before riding a moped or motorcycle on the road.

When the rider successfully completes CBT s/he or she will

get a Certificate of Completion (DL196) which is valid for three years. There is a power to request production of the DL 196.

The requirement to complete CBT does not apply to those riders who are:

(a) learning to ride a motorcycle and who have already obtained full moped entitlement as a result of passing a moped test on or after 1 December 1990; or
(b) riding a moped with full entitlement given automatically with a full car licence from 1 February 2001.

If learning to ride a moped or motorcycle, a pillion passenger cannot be carried.

A rider can only learn to ride on motorcycles over 125cc if:

(a) over 21 and accompanied by an approved instructor on a separate machine at all times; or
(b) riding a motorcycle with a sidecar.

Learner motorcyclists normally have to pass the written theory test as well as the practical test to gain a full motorcycle licence.

The New Category A and A1 Driving Licence At age 17 or over, the rider will have two types of full motorcycle licence to aim for - the A1 light motorcycle licence or the standard category A motorcycle licence.

To gain a full A1 light motorcycle licence the rider must successfully complete CBT and pass a theory test followed by a practical test on a vehicle between 75cc and 125cc. A full A1 licence permits him/her or her to ride any motorcycle up to 125cc and a power output of up to 11kw (14.6 bhp) without `L' plates, carry pillion passengers and use motorways.

To gain a full standard category A licence the rider must successfully complete CBT and pass a theory test followed by a practical test on a motorcycle of over 120cc but not larger than 125cc and capable of at least 100kph. A full standard category A licence permits a person to ride any motorcycle with a power output of up to 25kw (33bhp) and a power-to-weight ratio not exceeding 0.16kw/kg without 'L' plates, carry pillion passengers and use motorways. The rider is restricted to a motorcycle up to 25kw for two years (not counting any periods of disqualification). After two years s/he may ride any size motorcycle.

Direct Access for learner riders aged 21 or over Riders aged 21 or over may opt to take a test on a large motorcycle. On passing the test they are immediately qualified to ride any motorcycle without restrictions. This option is called Direct Access. The rider must complete CBT, and if necessary, a motorcycle theory test and a practical test on a motorcycle of at least 35kw (46.6bhp).

Accelerated Access If a rider has already obtained a full standard category A licence and has reached the age of 21 before the two year qualifying period is complete a third option is available. S/he may opt to take a further test on a motorcycle with a power output of at least 35kw (46.6bhp) to gain immediate access to all motorcycles. This is called Accelerated Access. The rider can practice for this test on motorcycles above 25kw only if accompanied by a certified motorcycle instructor on another motorcycle and displaying 'L' plates (see Training for Direct Access below). There is no need to complete CBT again, or pass another theory test.

Training for Direct Access or Accelerated Access So that learners aged 21 or over may practice for the large motorcycle test they may ride a motorcycle on the road that exceeds the UK learner specification, but only under the supervision of a certified Direct Access instructor. When learning on a large motorcycle the usual learner restrictions will apply ('L' plates, no pillion passengers and motorway prohibition).

■ 6. 'a motor vehicle, namely a ....'

This offence is committed by a learner rider who carries a passenger (with or without a sidecar). For the purpose of this example the offender was riding a 'learner motorcycle'. The offence could also have been committed on a moped, scooter or motor cycle.

'Moped' means a motor cycle which cannot go faster than 50 kilometres per hour (kph), with an engine not exceeding 50cc and if used before 1/8/1977 can be moved by pedals.

'Learner motorcycle' has an engine size up to 125cc and a power output of 11kilowatts (kw) or 14.6 brake horse power (bhp). The kw is the metric measurement of bhp. One bhp equals 0.75kw. Motor cycles over these limits are large motor cycles and can only be used by learners as explained above when training for Direct Access or Accelerated Access. There is no definition of scooter and it will fit into one of the above definitions.

■ 7. 'while carrying on it another person.'

This means carrying a pillion passenger or if fitted with a sidecar, a passenger in the sidecar. If carrying more than one passenger then besides this offence, the Construction and Use Regulations offence (reg 100) of using for an unsuitable purpose could also be considered.

(C) USUAL METHODS OF PROVING THESE POINTS

■ 1. to 5. as at Offence 14.

But care should be taken to ensure the correct licence is held to ride the particular motor cycle bearing in mind the age and experience of the rider as explained at (B) above.

■ 6. 'a motor vehicle, namely a ....'

This can be proved by identifying the class of motor cycle concerned either from the make and model, the description given by the rider, from the officer's own knowledge or from the registration document, etc. As shown above the deciding factors are the cc s and the power output in cases where it is difficult to classify a particular motor cycle.

■ 7. 'while carrying on it another person.'

This is usually proved in the reporting officer's statement of evidence that there were two persons on the motor cycle, eg 'Behind the rider was another person sitting astride the motor cycle, facing the front. The motor cycle was fitted with a seat and foot rests designed for a pillion passenger.'

(D) SUPPORTING EVIDENCE

If it can be proved that the pillion passenger knew the rider was only a learner, the passenger would most likely commit the offence of aiding and abetting the learner to carry a passenger.

The rider could be questioned as to whether the passenger was qualified to ride the motor cycle as this may help the court with any penalty. It is obviously more dangerous to carry a passenger who is not qualified than one who is qualified.

Care should be taken to deal with the passenger as a defendant or a witness. Only things said by the passenger in the presence and hearing of the defendant rider would be admissible under the 'hearsay' rule.

17. DRIVING WITH EXCESS ALCOHOL

Section 5(1) Road Traffic Act 1988

(A) POINTS TO PROVE

1. That you 2. did drive (or attempt to drive or were in charge of) 3. a certain motor vehicle, namely .... 4. on a road (or public place) called .... 5. after consuming so much alcohol that the proportion thereof in your breath (blood or urine) exceeds the prescribed limit.

(B) MEANING OF TERMS

■ 1. 'That you'

Means the person driving over the prescribed limit, ie the identity of the driver.

■ 2. 'did drive (or attempt to drive or were in charge of)'

'Attempting to drive' means that there must be an act substantially close to actually driving. Acts such as trying to start the engine, or a person who is sitting in the driving seat trying to put the vehicle in gear or 'revving up' the engine (even though the clutch had burnt out) *(R v Farrance* [1978] Crim LR 496) are examples of 'attempting to drive', provided there is an immediate intention of driving.

'In charge of' means that once a person takes a vehicle on a road or public place s/he normally remains in charge of that vehicle until s/he has taken it off the road or public place again. S/he will cease to be in charge where some intervening act occurs to remove the responsibility for being in charge from him. An example would be where someone else takes charge of the vehicle to such a degree that s/he will not resume control of the vehicle, such as where s/he gives his/her friend the ignition key and a taxi is ordered to take him/her home.

■ **3. 'a certain motor vehicle, namely ....'** See Glossary.

■ **4. 'on a road (or public place) called ....'**

See Glossary for 'road'. See also *Avery v CPS* [2011] EWHC 2388 (Admin). For a vehicle to be on a road it is not necessary for the vehicle to be in contact with the road surface: the boot extended over a road and a collision occurred.

'Public place' means any place to which the public have access, eg a farmer's field near a race course which is used for parking purposes on race days. This is so notwithstanding that the field could be closed at any time and that certain people could be refused admission. Generally a place is public if the majority of the public have access to it.

A place is private and this offence cannot be committed where only a minority group of the public are admitted.

For example where a field leading to a river could only be used, according to a sign, for 'Parking - Members of the Walton Angling Club only', it would constitute a private field. If the sign said 'Parking - No Caravans', then a restricted class cannot use the field, but as the majority group could use it, the field would be a public place.

■ **5. 'after consuming so much alcohol that the proportion thereof in your breath (blood or urine) exceeds the prescribed limit'.**

The prescribed limits at present are:
(a) 35 microgrammes of alcohol in 100 millilitres of breath;
(b) 80 milligrammes of alcohol in 100 millilitres of blood;
(c) 107 milligrammes of alcohol in 100 millilitres of urine.

(C) USUAL METHODS OF PROVING THESE POINTS

■ **1. 'That you'** See (C)1 of Offence 1.

■ **2. 'did drive (or attempt to drive or was in charge of)'**
See (C)2 of Offence 1 for 'drive'.

'Attempt to drive' can be proved by the officer in the case or another witness who saw the defendant attempting to drive. An admission on the part of the defendant would also help the prosecution case. Failing an admission, a question to the defendant such as, 'Where did you intend to go when you got into your car?' or, 'What were you trying to do?' etc, may help to prove that s/he had an intention to drive as discussed at point (B)2 of this offence.

The precise details of the evidence of attempting to drive that the officer or other witness saw must be shown in their statements of evidence.

'In charge of' can be proved by the police officer or other witness who saw the defendant near or sitting in the vehicle for example. Questions to determine whether the officer had taken any steps to prevent the defendant driving may be necessary, such as, 'Where are the ignition keys?' or, 'Is anybody else in charge of this vehicle?' See (D) of this offence for the statutory defence to being in charge.

■ **3. 'a certain motor vehicle, namely ....'**
See Glossary.

■ **4. 'on a road (or public place) called ....'**
See (C)4 of Offence 1 for 'road'.

To prove whether a place is 'public' could necessitate taking a statement from a person who had authorised access to a normally private place; enquiring about and keeping observations on the place to show actual usage; or describing any permanent or temporary signs that relate to who had access.

■ 5. 'after consuming so much alcohol the proportion thereof in your breath (blood or urine) exceeds the prescribed limit'.

Evidence of the proportion of alcohol in a specimen of breath, blood or urine may be by a document which is:

(a) a statement automatically produced by the breath analysis machine by which the proportion of alcohol in the breath specimen was measured and a certificate signed by a constable that the statement relates to a specimen provided by the accused at the date and time shown in the statement; and

(b) a certificate signed by an authorised analyst.

Where an analyst's findings are challenged by the defence, the prosecution could call the analyst to give evidence to explain his/her findings to the court.

(D) SUPPORTING EVIDENCE

Most police forces have produced a pro-forma to lead the officer in charge of the case through the procedure. The general idea with pro-formas is that they should be filled in as the procedure progresses in order to qualify as 'notes made at the time'. Such notes can be used to refresh memories and it has been found that a most accurate record of the investigation of OPL offences can thus be obtained.

Note 1. It is a defence for a person charged with 'Being in Charge' to prove that at the time s/he is alleged to have committed the offence the circumstances were such that there was no likelihood of his/her driving the vehicle while the proportion of alcohol in his/her breath, blood or urine remained likely to exceed the prescribed limit. However, in determining whether there was such a likelihood the court may disregard any injury to him/her and any damage to the vehicle.

The last part of this defence means that just because driving was impossible because of injury to him/her or damage to the vehicle, the court will not automatically find him/her not guilty. The court can disregard any injury or damage and still find that s/he was in charge of the vehicle. Note however that if a wheel clamp is fitted, this cannot be disregarded by the court as amounting to 'damage to the vehicle' (*Drake v DPP* [1994] Crim LR 855).

Note 2. A supervisor can aid and abet the learner to drive while over the prescribed limit etc. A conviction ensued where the supervisor had been drinking with the driver who was seen to swerve from side to side (*Crampton v Fish* (1969) 113 SJ 1003).

Note 3. Also consider, where appropriate, the offence of driving, attempting to drive or being in charge of a motor vehicle on a road or public place while unfit to drive through drink or drugs. 'Drugs' include any intoxicant other than alcohol, therefore even solvent abuse may be covered by this offence.

Note 4. The offence of obstructing the police under section 89(2) of the Police Act 1996 may be appropriate where the accused deliberately obstructs the police officers in the execution of their duty.

Note 5: Section 154 of SOCPA 2005 provides new powers to take evidential samples at a place other than a police station when suitable equipment is available, Section 6D(1A)(2A) Road Traffic Act 1988.

Note 6. *Chalupa v CPS* [2009] All ER (D) 09 (Nov). It is well established that, only in exceptional circumstances where a solicitor is readily available, can a breath test be delayed to allow an individual to take legal advice, as there is a public interest that a test be undertaken promptly.

18. FAILURE TO WEAR A SEAT BELT

Regulation 5 of the Motor Vehicles (Wearing of Seat Belts) Regulations 1993 and section 14 of the Road Traffic Act 1988

(A) POINTS TO PROVE

1. That you 2. did drive/were a passenger 3. in a motor vehicle 4. on a road 5. while not wearing a prescribed type of adult belt.

(B) MEANING OF TERMS

■ 1. 'That you'

Means the person driving or the passenger, ie the identity and not being a person under the age of 14 years.

■ 2. 'Did drive/were a passenger'

See Glossary for 'drive'. Passenger means carried in the vehicle, ie riding in the front seat of a motor vehicle (other than a two wheeled motor cycle with or without a sidecar) or riding in the rear seat of a motor car or a passenger car which is not a motor car.

■ 3. 'In a motor vehicle' (which is not a two wheeled motor cycle with or without sidecar)

See Glossary for 'motor vehicle'.

■ 4. 'on a road' See Glossary.

■ 5. 'while not wearing a prescribed type of adult belt'.

This point means a seat belt as defined, ie in these Regulations, 'adult belt' means a seat belt in respect of which one or more of the following requirements is satisfied, namely, that:

(a) it is a three-point belt which has been marked in accordance with regulation 47(7) of the Construction and Use Regulations;
(b) it is a lap belt which has been so marked;
(c) it is a seat belt that falls within regulation 47(4)(c)(i) or (ii) of those Regulations;
(d) it is a seat belt fitted in a relevant vehicle ('the vehicle in question') and comprised in a restraint system -

(i) of a type which has been approved by an authority of another Member State for use by all persons who are aged 13 years or more or are of 150cm or more in height, and

(ii) in respect of which, by virtue of such approval, the requirements of the law of another Member State corresponding to these Regulations would be met were it to be worn by persons who are either aged 13 years or more or of 150 centimetres or more in height when travelling in the vehicle in question in that State.

The interpretation of references to relevant vehicles:

(1) In these Regulations 'relevant vehicle' means -

(a) a passenger car,

(b) a light goods vehicle, or

(c) a small bus.

(2) For the purposes of this regulation -

'light goods vehicle' means a goods vehicle which -

(a) has four or more wheels,

(b) has a maximum design speed exceeding 25km per hour,

(c) has a maximum laden weight not exceeding 3.5 tonnes;

'small bus' means a motor vehicle which -

(a) is constructed or adapted for use for the carriage of passengers and is not a goods vehicle,

(b) has more than eight seats in addition to the driver's seat,

(c) has four or more wheels,

(d) has a maximum design speed exceeding 25km per hour,

(e) has a maximum laden weight not exceeding 3.5 tonnes,

(f) is not constructed or adapted for the carriage of standing passengers.

(C) USUAL METHODS OF PROVING THESE POINTS

■ **1. 'That you'** See (C)1 of Offence 1.

■ **2. 'did drive/were a passenger'**

These points can be proved by the police officer's observations in his/her statement of evidence.

■ **3. 'in a motor vehicle'** See Glossary.

■ **4. 'on a road'**

See Glossary, also C4 of Offence 1'.

■ **5. 'while not wearing a prescribed type of adult belt'.**

This point can be proved in the majority of cases by the observations of the reporting officer.

Where there is any doubt as to whether the seat belt is as prescribed, regulation 47 of the Construction and Use Regulations will have to be consulted.

Normally the following sentence in the reporting officer's statement will suffice: 'The seat belt was fitted and was in good working order when I tested it. I saw that the driver (passenger) was not wearing it.'

(D) SUPPORTING EVIDENCE

Note 1. Be aware of the following exemptions in regulation 6.

(1) The requirements of regulation 5 do not apply to:

- (a) a person holding a medical certificate;
- (b) a person using a vehicle constructed or adapted for the delivery of goods or mail to consumers or addresses, as the case may be, while engaged in making local rounds of deliveries or collections;
- (c) a person driving a vehicle while performing a manoeuvre which includes reversing;
- (d) a qualified driver (within the meaning given by regulation 17 of the Motor Vehicles (Driving Licences) Regulations 1999) who is supervising the holder of a provisional licence (within the meaning of Part III of the Act) while that holder is performing a manoeuvre which includes reversing;
- (e) a person by whom, as provided in the Motor Vehicles (Driving Licences) Regulations 1999, a test of competence to drive is being conducted and his/her wearing a seat belt would endanger him/herself or any other person;

(f) a person driving or riding in a vehicle while it is being used for fire brigade or police purposes or for carrying a person in lawful custody (a person who is being so carried being included in this exemption);

(fa/fb)persons using for Serious Organised Crime purposes;

(g) the driver of -

  (i) a licensed taxi while it is being used for seeking hire, or answering a call for hire, or carrying a passenger for hire, or

  (ii) a private hire vehicle while it is being used to carry a passenger for hire;

(h) a person riding in a vehicle being used under a trade licence, for the purpose of investigating or remedying a mechanical fault in the vehicle;

(j) a disabled person wearing a disabled person's belt; or

(k) a person riding in a vehicle while it is taking part in a procession organised by or on behalf of the Crown.

(2) Without prejudice to paragraph (1)(k), the requirements of regulation 5 do not apply to a person riding in a vehicle which is taking part in a procession held to mark or commemorate an event if either:

  (a) the procession is one commonly or customarily held in the police area or areas in which it is being held; or

  (b) notice in respect of the procession was given in accordance with section 11 of the Public Order Act 1986.

(3) The requirements of regulation 5 do not apply to:

  (a) a person driving a vehicle if the driver's seat is not provided with an adult belt;

  (b) a person riding in the front of a vehicle if no adult belt is available for him/her in the front of the vehicle;

  (c) a person riding in the rear of a vehicle if no adult belt is available for him/her in the rear of the vehicle.

Also see Schedule 2 of these Regulations for further interpretation regarding availability of seat belts.

Note 2. The seat belt law for children (under the age of 14) can be found at section 15 Road Traffic Act 1988, the Motor Vehicles (Wearing of Seat Belts) Regulations 1993 and the Motor Vehicles (Wearing of Seat Belts by Children in Front Seats) Regulations 1993 (as amended by Statutory Instrument 2006/1892&2213, in force 18.9.06). Where a child (under 14) is a front seat or a rear seat passenger (providing a rear seat belt is fitted) the driver will commit an offence unless the child is wearing a seat belt or other restraint conforming with the Regulations.
Note 3. A 14- or 15-year-old offender cannot be fined if they fail to pay a fixed penalty. It is suggested reporting them for summons for consideration by a Youth Court.

19. DANGEROUS PARTS

Regulation 100(1) Road Vehicles (Construction and Use) Regulations 1986, and s40A Road Traffic Act 1988

(A) POINTS TO PROVE

1. That you 2. did use (or cause, or permit to be used) 3. on a road called .... 4. a certain motor vehicle namely a .... (or trailer drawn by a motor vehicle) 5. a part (or accessory) of which, namely .... (specify) 6. was in such condition, that danger was caused 7. or was likely to be caused to persons in or on that vehicle (or trailer) or on a road in that .... (specify defect).

(B) MEANING OF TERMS

- **1. 'That you'** Means the identity of the person using, causing or permitting the use of the motor vehicle.
- **2. 'did use (or cause, or permit to be used)'** See Glossary.
- **3. 'on a road called ....'** See Glossary.
- **4. 'a certain motor vehicle namely a ......' (or trailer drawn by a motor vehicle).** See Glossary for 'motor vehicle' and 'trailer'.

■ 5. 'a part (or accessory) of which ....'

Means that such things as doors, windows and wings are parts, and such things as wing mirrors, windscreen wipers and roof racks are accessories.

A tow chain has been held not to be a 'part' (*Jenkins v Deane* (1933) 103 LJKB 250), but a tow bar connecting a vehicle and a trailer together has been held to come within the regulation where the joining was defective (*O'Neill v Brown* [1961] 1 QB 420).

■ 6. 'was in such condition, that danger was caused'

This point means that the condition caused danger or in other words injured someone. For example where a hole appears in the wing of a car and a pedestrian is cut by the sharp rusty edges of the hole, then danger is caused.

In *Reeve v Webb* (1972) 117 SJ 127 it was held that alterations to exhaust pipes fall within another part of this regulation.

■ 7. 'or was likely to be caused to persons in or on hat vehicle (or trailer) or on a road in that .... (specify defect)'.

'Likely to be caused' means potentially dangerous. Examples would be sharp edges jutting from the body of a motor vehicle; a loose driver's seat which could lead to loss of control of the vehicle; projecting wheel wing nuts or mudguards which could strike a pedestrian; a loose rear bumper which may fall off and cause an accident.

'To persons in or on that vehicle (or trailer)' means that the danger or potential danger is sufficient if it applies to passengers or even the driver of the motor vehicle concerned.

'Or on a road' covers potential danger or actual danger to pedestrians or anyone not actually in or on the offending motor vehicle.

'In that .... (specify defect)' means that the offence must show what parts and accessories are not maintained in good condition (*Simmons v Fowler* (1950) 48 LGR 623).

(C) USUAL METHODS OF PROVING THESE POINTS

■ **1. 'That you'** See (C)1 of Offence 1.

■ **2. 'did use (or cause, or permit to be used)'** (C)2 Offence 5. In the case of 'use' for construction and use offences there is an absolute prohibition on the part of the employer. If an offence is committed and the employer was quite unaware of any defect s/he is still liable for 'using' (*Green v Burnett* [1954] 3 All ER 273). Therefore, to prove the offence of using against the employer as well as against the driver, the employer must be interviewed and questioned as follows:

'Are you (or your firm) the owner of motor vehicle ....?' Then, 'Was the vehicle being used on your (or your firm's) business at ..... (time) ..... on ..... (date) ..... in ..... (road) .....?'

For the offence of 'using' these questions must receive the answer 'Yes'. While it is not necessary to prove the employer knew of any defect it is good evidence for the prosecution if s/he admits s/he did.

■ **3. 'on a road called ....'** See (C)4 of Offence 1.

■ **4. 'a certain motor vehicle namely a ....' (or trailer drawn by a motor vehicle)'** See Glossary, and for trailer a witnesses description of the trailer and coupling would suffice.

■ **5. 'a part (or accessory) of which, namely ....' (specify)** This point can be proved by the police officer dealing with the case describing the item in question in his/her statement of evidence, eg 'The front nearside wing was badly corroded .... etc'. Specific details of the defective parts and/or accessories must be given in the charge and therefore in the prosecution evidence (*Simmons v Fowler* (1950) 48 LGR 623).

■ **6. 'was in such condition, that danger was caused'** This point is proved, firstly by the prosecution witness (most likely the police officer) examining the personal injury and describing it in his/her evidence. Secondly, a statement from the injured party detailing the injury and how it was caused would be required.

■ 7. 'or was likely to be caused to persons in or on that vehicle (or trailer) or on a road in that .... (specify defect).

Where no injury is caused, the above element has to be proved. This is usually done by the subjective judgment of the officer concerned. Namely, a sentence in the police officer's statement of evidence to the effect that 'Should anyone come into contact with the jagged metal on the front nearside wing they would be injured', or, 'If a pedestrian collided with the piece of metal left after the front nearside wing mirror had broken off, s/he would be injured'. The court will then use its judgment regarding the proof of potential danger.

(D) SUPPORTING EVIDENCE

Note. Several other offences are included in the above Regulations but are not quite so common as the offence outlined. The other offences include the number and manner of carrying of passengers being dangerous or potentially dangerous; insecure or dangerous load; and using a motor vehicle for an unsuitable purpose. Note that regulation 100 is not endorsable but section 40A of the Road Traffic Act 1988 is endorsable.

20. DEFECTIVE BRAKES

Regulation 18 Road Vehicles (Construction and Use) Regulations 1986 and s41A Road Traffic Act 1988

(A) POINTS TO PROVE

1. That you 2. did use (or cause or permit to be used) 3. on a road called ....
4. a motor vehicle, namely a .... (or trailer)
5. on which a part of (the means of operation of) the braking system fitted thereto
6. was not maintained in good and efficient working order and properly adjusted.

(B) MEANING OF TERMS

■ 1. 'That you'

Means the identity of the person using, causing or permitting the use.

■ 2. 'did use (or cause or permit to be used)' See Glossary.

■ 3. 'on a road called' See Glossary.

■ 4. 'a motor vehicle, namely a .... (or trailer)'

See Glossary for 'motor vehicle' and 'trailer'.

■ 5. 'on which a part of (the means of operation of) the braking system fitted thereto'

This point means that 'a part', eg the brake shoes or brake pads were not maintained and/or the 'means of operation' such as the hand brake lever ratchet or the cable (if fitted) was not maintained. It was held in *Kennett v British Airports Authority* [1975] Crim LR 106 that every part of the braking system and of the means of operation must be maintained etc. Note that a brake drum is part of the wheel and not the braking system.

■ 6. 'was not maintained in good efficient working order and properly adjusted'.

This point means an absolute requirement for a person to maintain his/her brakes to escape liability. It is insufficient to show that the brakes were regularly maintained. 'Not maintained' usually includes worn, seized or rusted parts etc and 'not properly adjusted' includes stretched cables or inoperative self-adjusting ratchets on drum brakes etc.

(C) USUAL METHODS OF PROVING THESE POINTS

■ 1. 'That you'

See (C)1 of Offence 1.

■ 2. 'did use (or cause or permit to be used)'

See (C)2 of Offence 5.

In the case of 'use' for construction and use offences see (C)2 of Offence 19.

■ **3. 'on a road called ....'** See (C)4 of Offence 1.

■ **4. 'a motor vehicle, namely a .... (or trailer)'**

See Glossary, and for trailer, a witnesses description of the trailer and coupling would suffice.

■ **5. 'on which a part of (the means of operation of) the braking system, fitted thereto'**

This point can be proved by showing the brakes don't work by using a simple test such as pushing the vehicle along the road with the brake(s) set. If a vehicle examiner who has been authorised by a chief constable examines the brakes his/her evidence will show a more detailed inspection and will probably name the 'part' concerned.

Note that an officer who is not authorised to test and inspect will have to ask the driver before carrying out his/her examination. If permission is refused s/he can hold the vehicle until an authorised examiner arrives where s/he feels it would be dangerous for the vehicle to proceed. If the driver still refuses to wait s/he commits a further possible offence. See 'Powers' at the end of the book for - seizure of vehicles where no driving licence or insurance - and possible arrest of suspect to prevent injury to self or another.

■ **6. 'was not maintained in good and efficient working order and properly adjusted'.**

This point is proved along with the last point. Obviously defective parts such as broken brake cable, leaking hydraulic fluid, or a handbrake that won't catch on its ratchet etc, can be proved by the observations of almost anyone. Where an accident is caused by alleged brake failure, or other more technical circumstances arise, the services of a trained vehicle examiner may be required. The most common brake defects are worn shoes and pads, seized cylinders and poor adjustment. In *Stoneley v Richardson* [1973] RTR 229 it was held that defective brakes do not have to be proved by an authorised examiner. Provided the defendant consents to the test or inspection the person examining the brakes (usually a constable) does not need to be an authorised examiner.

Inefficiency etc is sometimes proved by the use of an instrument which measures braking efficiency, called a Tapley meter.

(D) SUPPORTING EVIDENCE

A practical consideration when testing vehicle parts is for the defendant to be asked to operate the part, such as brakes, him/herself. In this way an allegation to the effect that the officer did not apply the brake correctly may be quickly dealt with by saying, 'After I [the officer] tested the brakes and found the handbrake to be defective I asked the defendant to apply the handbrake. S/he did so but could not get it to work.'

Note 1. A latent defect amounting to a dangerous condition is not a defence but would be good mitigation, *F Austin (Leyton) Ltd v East* [1961] Crim LR 119. The facts of this case showed that there was no negligence but nevertheless such offences are absolute.

21. DEFECTIVE WINDSCREEN WIPERS

Regulation 34(6) Road Vehicles (Construction and Use) Regulations 1986 and section 42 of the Road Traffic Act 1988

(A) POINTS TO PROVE

1. That you 2. did use (or cause or permit to be used) 3. on a road called .... 4. a motor vehicle, namely a .... 5. on which the windscreen wiper was not maintained in good and efficient working order, and/or properly adjusted.

(B) MEANING OF TERMS

■ 1. 'That you'

Means the person's identity.

■ **2. 'did use (or cause or permit to be used)'** See Glossary.
■ **3. 'on a road called ....'** See Glossary.
■ **4. 'a motor vehicle, namely a ....'**
See Glossary.
■ **5. 'on which the windscreen wiper was not maintained in good and efficient working order and/or properly adjusted'.**
The point means that the switch, the motor or the arms or blades were defective or missing etc. Common faults are wiper blades missing or the electric motor failing.

(C) USUAL METHODS OF PROVING THESE POINTS

■ **1. 'That you'**
See (C)1 of Offence 1.
■ **2. 'did use (or cause or permit to be used)'**
See (C)2 of Offences 5 and 19.
3. 'on a road called ....'
See (C)4 of Offence 1.
■ **4. 'a motor vehicle, namely a ....'**
See Glossary.
■ **5. 'on which the windscreen wiper was not maintained in good and efficient working order and/or properly adjusted'.**
This point can be proved simply by testing the wipers and getting no response. Where the motor is working the offence can still be committed where the arm or blade is missing. The defendant should also be asked to operate the wipers to avoid allegations to the effect that the wipers were not switched on correctly.

(D) SUPPORTING EVIDENCE

Note 1. Depending on the make of motor vehicle, normally there are two wipers fitted and both must work as regulation 34(1) of the above regulation insists that 'an adequate view of the road in front of the near and offsides of the vehicle...' is required. But this is the general position and in vehicles like Minis it could be argued that such a view can be obtained when only the wiper in front of the driver works, therefore each vehicle must be dealt with separately.

Note 2. Regulation 34(1) states that if a view to the front can be obtained without looking through the windscreen, wipers are not required. Only old vehicles pre about 1940 and the occasional newer vehicle such as some Land Rovers have the front opening windscreens.

22. DEFECTIVE SILENCER

Regulation 54(1) Road Vehicles (Construction and Use) Regulations 1986 and section 42 of the Road Traffic Act 1988

(A) POINTS TO PROVE

1. That you 2. did use (or cause or permit to be used) 3. on a road called .... 4. a vehicle propelled by an internal combustion engine, namely a ....
5. so that the exhaust gases from the engine escaped into the atmosphere without first passing through the silencer, expansion chamber or other contrivance required to be fitted by the Motor Vehicles (Construction and Use) Regulations.

(B) MEANING OF TERMS

■ 1. 'That you'

Means the identity of the person using the motor vehicle etc.

■ 2. 'did use (or cause or permit to be used)'

See Glossary.

■ 3. 'on a road called ....'

See Glossary.

■ 4. a vehicle propelled by an internal combustion engine, namely a ....'

See Glossary.

As the majority of vehicles are propelled in this manner, this point speaks for itself.

■ 5. 'so that the exhaust gases from the engine escaped into the atmosphere without first passing through the silencer, expansion chamber or other contrivance required to be fitted by the Motor Vehicles (Construction and Use) Regulations'

This point means for example that the gases from the engine escape from the faulty manifold (which is at the exit point adjacent to the engine) or a broken front pipe, a broken expansion chamber or from the silencer (provided this occurs before they pass through it). These regulations require that either a silencer, expansion chamber or other contrivance is fitted as may be reasonable to reduce the noise. If an exhaust system has two such articles this offence is not committed if the gases pass through any such article before escaping into the atmosphere.

(C) USUAL METHODS OF PROVING THESE POINTS

■ 1. 'That you'

See (C)1 of Offence 1.

■ 2. 'did use (or cause or permit to be used)'

See (C)2 of Offences 5 and 19.

■ 3. 'on a road called ....'

See (C)4 of Offence 1.

■ 4. 'a vehicle propelled by an internal combustion engine, namely a ....'

This point can be proved by describing the vehicle in the statement of the police officer who is dealing with the case, eg, 'I caused the defendant, John Smith to stop the Ford saloon motor car registered number .... etc'.

■ 5. 'so that the exhaust gases from the engine escaped into the atmosphere without first passing through the silencer, expansion chamber or other contrivance required to be fitted by the Motor Vehicles (Construction and Use) Regulations'.

This point can be proved by inspecting the silencer system with the engine running and watching where the gases are escaping. In the vast majority of cases the exhaust pipe corrodes around the bend which goes over the rear axle on motor cars or that particular pipe breaks away from the end of the silencer.

However, there is no offence against this regulation if only the tail pipe (ie the piece leading the gases into the atmosphere from the end of the silencer which is the furthest from the engine) is defective, as the gases will have passed through the silencer.

(D) SUPPORTING EVIDENCE

Motor cycles owners have been known to remover the baffle plates of the silencer to make the engine sound bigger and 'sporty'. A way of proving this is to push a retractable steel rule (a useful item for a police officer to carry) up the exhaust pipe and into the silencer. If the rule passes through the silencer unhindered, suitable questions could be put to the rider to prove a regulation 54(2) offence.

Note. The further offence of failing to maintain such a system is contrary to regulation 54(2) of these Regulations. This offence can be considered where a hole appears in the side of the silencer etc, as some doubt exists whether the gases have passed 'through' the silencer etc, if they have passed through half of the silencer, Until there is judicial assistance to say that such gases must pass all the way through a silencer to escape liability under regulation 54(1), a regulation 54(2) offence may be the safest offence.

23. DEFECTIVE TYRES

Regulation 27(1) (or (4)) Road Vehicles (Construction and Use) Regulations 1986 and section 41A of the Road Traffic Act 1988

(A) POINTS TO PROVE

1. That you 2. used (or caused or permitted to be used) 3. on a road called .... 4. a motor vehicle (or trailer), namely a .... 5. fitted with a pneumatic tyre 6. whose grooves of the tread pattern of the tyre did not have a depth of at least 1. 6 mm throughout a continuous band situated in the central three-quarters of the breadth of the tread and round the entire outer circumference of the tyre.

(B) MEANING OF TERMS

■ 1. 'That you'

Means the identity of the person using the motor vehicle etc.

■ 2. 'used (or caused or permitted to be used)'

■ 3. 'on a road called ....'

■ 4. 'a motor vehicle (or trailer) namely a ....'

With effect from 1 January 1992 the 'old' offences at paragraphs (f) and (g) of regulation 27(1) of the 1986 Regulations no longer apply to passenger motor cars other than motor cars constructed or adapted to carry no more than eight seated passengers in addition to the driver, or to goods vehicles with a maximum gross weight which does not exceed 3,500 kg. The new offence applies to motor cars and goods vehicles other than those shown above and also applies to light trailers first used on or after 3 January 1993, ie, a trailer with a maximum gross weight not exceeding 3,500kg.

In other words the old offences under (f) and (g) above now apply to motor cars with eight or more seats or goods vehicles 3,500 kg or under and to the other categories of vehicle not mentioned here.

The new offence under regulation 27(4)(d)(f) (which contains the same requirement of 1.6mm minimum depth throughout a continuous band of three-quarters of the breadth) applies to the vast majority of motor cars and trailers and goods vehicles of 3,500kg or under.

■ 5. 'fitted with a pneumatic tyre'

Pneumatic tyre means inflatable as opposed to the early tyre or solid tyres.

■ 6. 'whose grooves on the tread pattern did not have a depth of at least 1. 6mm throughout a continuous band situated in the central three-quarters of the breadth of the tread and round the entire outer circumference of the tyre'.

'Tread pattern' means the raised and lowered pattern which, in modern tyres, is provided around the walls of the tyre to a small degree as well as where the tyre makes contact with the road surface. 'Tread' is the part of the tyre which comes into contact with the road surface in normal driving, ie not when cornering at speed.

Therefore, this point means that the tyre did not have a 1.6mm depth of tread pattern grooves around the tyre in a continuous band situated in the central three-quarters of the width of the tread. It follows that if there is a small bald patch (or a patch with grooves less than 1.6mm deep) 4cm in diameter on a tread width of 12cm an offence is committed, for 4 cm is more than a quarter of the 12cm width of tread. It is important to note that the bald patch or the patch without the 1.6mm depth of tread grooves is not required to go right around the tyre.

It is sufficient to contravene this regulation where the patch is more than a quarter of the breadth of the tread, because there cannot be at least three-quarters of good tread around the whole circumference of the tyre in such a case.

It should be noted that the required three-quarters width of 1.6mm tread pattern grooves should be in a continuous band.

Therefore, where the tread is below 1.6mm depth in the middle of the tread and around the circumference of the tyre it is no good the defendant adding up the 'bits' on either side of the worn part to try to make a good three-quarters.

(C) USUAL METHODS OF PROVING THESE POINTS

■ 1. 'That you'

See (C)1 of Offence 1.

■ 2. 'used (or caused or permitted to be used)'

See (C)2 of Offences 5 and 19.

■ 3. 'on a road called ....'

See (C)4 of Offence 1.

■ 4. 'a motor vehicle (or trailer), namely a ....'

Proof of the number of seats in a passenger motor car or the maximum gross weight of a goods vehicle may be necessary to show this new offence applies to the vehicle in question. For example: 'The motor car had been adapted to carry [8 - or specify] seated passengers (but not more than [8 - or specify]) in addition to the driver.' 'The goods vehicle was ....[specify weight].'

■ 5. 'fitted with a pneumatic tyre'

This point is proved by describing the tyre in question, eg, 'The front nearside tyre was a radial, such and such a make, size 165 x 14 and was designed as a tubeless tyre'. It is important for the prosecution case to try to identify the tyre by taking the tyre or batch number which will usually be something like 824927 16E, on the tyre wall in letters and figures about 1 cm high - in about a quarter of all checks the number is non-existent or illegible and the police officer should try to remember other forms of identification such as marks or scratches etc on the tyre. This precaution may well deter a dishonest defendant bringing a totally different tyre to court and alleging that the officer was mistaken as the tyre was within the law.

■ 6. 'whose grooves of the tread pattern of the tyre did not have a depth of at least 1. 6 mm throughout a continuous band situated in the central three-quarters of the breadth of the tread and round the entire outer circumference of the tyre'.

This point is proved beyond any doubt when a completely bald patch exceeding a quarter of the breadth of the tread is present. In the other case where the depth of the tread pattern grooves is in issue an approved measuring device can be used.

(D) SUPPORTING EVIDENCE

Each tyre must be treated as a separate entity and separate information must be laid where offences concern more than one tyre *(Saines v Woodhouse* [1970] 2 All ER 388). This includes double tyres on lorries and close coupled wheels.

Note 1. In the case of *Stoneley v Richardson* [1973] Crim LR 310 it was held that it does not matter whether or not the constable who inspected the tyre was an authorised examiner under section 67 Road Traffic Act 1988. Where the constable is not authorised the defendant could have allowed the constable to carry out the inspection.

Note 2. The further offences under regulation 27 should be considered. These are regulation 27(1) (a) to (h) with the exception of (f) and (g). Further offences include tyres not maintained in good order, with defects such as cuts, bulges, lumps, tears or exposed ply or cord; wrongly inflated tyres or tyres put to the wrong use; recut pneumatic tyres where the ply or cord has been exposed, or those recut in a pattern other than to the manufacturer's specification.

Note 3. Vehicles exceeding capacity for eight seated passengers or 3,500kg require at least 1mm of tread.

Note 4. Be aware of exempted vehicles such as agricultural trailers and pedestrian controlled works trucks.

24. QUITTING WITHOUT STOPPING ENGINE AND SETTING BRAKE

Regulation 107(1) Road Vehicles (Construction and Use) Regulations 1986, and section 42 Road Traffic Act 1988

(A) POINTS TO PROVE

1. That you 2. did leave, cause (or permit) to be left
3. on a road called .... 4. a motor vehicle, namely a .... 5. which was not attended
6. by a person duly licensed to drive it
7. without the engine being stopped and/or
8. without the parking brake being effectively set.

(B) MEANING OF TERMS

■ 1. 'That you'

Means the person quitting the vehicle.

■ 2. 'did leave, cause (or permit) to be left'

See Glossary.

■ 3. 'on a road called ....'

See Glossary.

■ 4. 'a motor vehicle, namely a ....'

See Glossary.

Notable exceptions include police, fire brigade and ambulance purposes, and vehicles which require the engine to run to operate special machinery or apparatus such as a gully emptying vehicle.

■ 5. 'which was not attended'

Means there is no person able to keep it under observation and reach it in time to prevent anything untoward happening (*Starfire Diamond Rings Ltd v Angel* (1962) 106 SJ 854 and *Ingleton of Ilford Ltd v General Accident & Co* [1967] 2 Lloyd's Rep 179).

■ 6. 'by a person duly licensed to drive it'

This means that if anyone is in attendance at the vehicle, to escape committing an offence under this regulation s/he must be the holder of a current driving licence for that class of vehicle.

■ 7. 'without the engine being stopped'

This point means that, apart from the exceptions at regulation 107(2)(a) and (b) (the main ones are shown at point 4 above), the engines of all motor vehicles must be stopped when the vehicles are unattended.

■ 8. 'without the parking brake being effectively set'.

Means that the handbrake (in the case of a saloon motor car) was not set. The driver could have applied the brake but because of a defective ratchet, for instance, the brake could have slipped and as a result would not be effectively set.

(C) USUAL METHODS OF PROVING THESE POINTS

■ 1. 'That you'

See (C)1 of Offence 1.

■ 2. 'did leave, cause (or permit) to be left'

See (C)2 of Offence 5.

■ 3. 'on a road called ....'

See (C)4 of Offence 1.

■ 4. 'a motor vehicle, namely a ....'

See Glossary.

■ 5. 'which was not attended'

Generally this point is proved by the officer finding an unattended vehicle with the engine running. After making unsuccessful inquiries to find the driver in the immediate area, these facts can be used to prove the unattended element.

■ 6. 'by a person duly licensed to drive it'

The problem of 'hearsay evidence' can occur where a passenger in a motor vehicle has to be asked whether or not s/he holds a current licence for the class of vehicle.

A way round this hearsay evidence is for the officer to say, for example: 'The passenger Mr Jones says he is not licensed to drive this car so I am reporting you (the defendant) for quitting a vehicle' etc.

If the passenger is not in possession of a licence, but states s/he is the holder of the necessary licence, further inquiries will be made by the police officer to ascertain whether or not s/he is a duly licensed driver. If not, the defendant driver can be seen later and told s/he will be reported.

■ 7. 'without the engine being stopped'

This point can be proved by the observations of the officer dealing, namely, 'The engine was running, ignition key switched on, exhaust fumes coming from exhaust pipe' etc.

■ 8. 'without the parking brake being effectively set'.

This point can be proved by pushing the vehicle along the road to show there was no braking effect; by events speaking for themselves in cases where the unattended vehicle runs away down hill; and by observing the handbrake lever in the off position etc.

Failing to set the handbrake is sometimes detected when it is too late, ie when a vehicle has been parked unattended and has then begun to move and run away downhill, perhaps resulting in an accident. In such a case a careful examination of the handbrake should be made bearing this offence in mind.

If necessary the prosecution might call a vehicle examiner to give evidence where there is some technical failure of the handbrake such as a worn ratchet causing the brake lever to slip or a frayed cable which snapped under pressure.

(D) SUPPORTING EVIDENCE

Note. A person failing to set the handbrake can also be reported for leaving a vehicle in a dangerous position contrary to section 22 Road Traffic Act 1988.

25. HORNS NOT FITTED

Regulation 37 Road Vehicles (Construction and Use) Regs 1986 and section 42 Road Traffic Act 1988

(A) POINTS TO PROVE

1. That you 2. did use (or cause or permit to be used) 3. on a road called .... 4. a motor vehicle namely a .... 5. which was not fitted 6. with an instrument capable of giving audible and sufficient warning of its approach or position.

(B) MEANING OF TERMS

■ 1. 'That you'

This point means the identity of the person using, causing or permitting to be used.

■ 2. 'did use (or cause or permit to be used)'

See Glossary.

■ 3. 'on a road called ....'

See Glossary.

■ 4. 'a motor vehicle namely a ....'

See Glossary. The vehicle must have a maximum speed of more than 20mph.

■ 5. 'which was not fitted'

This point means that either the motor vehicle in question had no horn fitted at all or that the one that was fitted did not conform to the requirements of the next point.

■ 6. 'with an instrument capable of giving audible and sufficient warning of its approach or position'.

This point means that the horn if not fitted would hardly be able to warn people. If fitted it has got to work sufficiently well to warn other road users of its approach etc. Therefore horns with loose wires where the sound emitted is not continuous and reliable or where the sound is too soft, etc would not comply with this regulation.

(C) USUAL METHODS OF PROVING THESE POINTS

■ **1. 'That you'** See (C)1 of Offence 1.

■ **2. 'did use (or cause or permit to be used)'**

See (C)2 of offence 5, and in the case of 'use' for construction and use offences see (C)2 of Offence 19.

■ **3. 'on a road called ....'** See (C)4 of Offence 1.

■ **4. 'a motor vehicle namely a ....'** See Glossary.

■ **5. 'which was not fitted'**

This point is proved by an examination of the motor vehicle, which in these days of mass produced cars will generally reveal that a horn is fitted. In a few cases where a horn has been removed this can be proved by stating so or by an admission on the part of the defendant. In most cases the horn will be fitted and although it is not necessary to prove why the horn didn't work when operated it may be of assistance to the court.

In practice it is better to show in evidence for the prosecution that the defendant was also asked to try to get the horn to work as explained at point (D)(b) of offence 20.

■ **6. 'with an instrument capable of giving audible and sufficient warning of its approach or position'**

This point is proved by no sound or insufficient sound being emitted when the horn, if any, is tested. Common sense will prevail as to whether the noise emitted is sufficient or not.

(D) SUPPORTING EVIDENCE

Note. Several points of interest relating to horns are dealt with at other parts of regulation 37 as below.

(4) Subject to paragraphs (5) (6) and (7) no motor vehicle shall be fitted with a gong, bell, siren or two-tone horn.

(5) The following vehicles may be fitted with a gong, bell, siren or two-tone horn:

  (a) motor vehicles used for fire brigade, ambulance or police purposes;

  (b) motor vehicles owned by a body formed primarily for

fire salvage and used for those or similar purposes;
(c) motor vehicles owned by the Forestry Commission or by local authorities and used from time to time for the purpose of fighting fires;
(d) motor vehicles owned by the Secretary of State for Defence and used for the purposes of the disposal of bombs or explosives;
(e) motor vehicles used for the purposes of the Blood Transfusion Service provided under the National Health Service Act 1977 or under the National Health Service (Scotland) Act 1947;
(f) motor vehicles used by Her Majesty's Coastguard or the Coastguard Auxiliary Service to aid persons in danger or vessels in distress on or near the coast;
(g) motor vehicles owned by the [National Coal Board] and used for the purposes of rescue operations at mines;
(h) motor vehicles owned by the Secretary of State for Defence and used by the Royal Air Force Mountain Rescue Service for rescue operations in connection with crashed aircraft or any other emergencies; and
(i) motor vehicles owned by the Royal National Lifeboat Institution and used for launching lifeboats.

(6) The provisions of paragraphs (2) and (4) above shall not apply so as to make it unlawful for a motor vehicle to be fitted with an instrument or apparatus other than a two-tone horn designed to emit a sound for the purpose of informing members of the public that goods are on the vehicle for sale. Colonel Bogey type horns and other such ditties are now unlawful on vehicles first used on or after August 1, 1973.

Further paragraphs deal with bells, gongs or sirens being used for theft prevention purposes or to summons help for the conductors, drivers and inspectors of large passenger-carrying vehicles. Regulation 37(2) requires that the sound emitted by any horn (other than a reversing alarm or two-tone horn) fitted to a wheeled vehicle first used on or after 1 August 1973, shall be continuous and uniform and not strident.

26. PEDESTRIAN FAILING TO COMPLY WITH CONSTABLE'S DIRECTION

Section 37 Road Traffic Act 1988

(A) POINTS TO PROVE

1. That you 2. being a person on foot 3. where a police constable (or a traffic warden) in uniform 4. was engaged in the regulation of vehicular traffic in a road 5. did proceed across (or along) the carriageway 6. in contravention of a direction to stop given by the constable (or the traffic warden) in the execution of his/her duty.

(B) MEANING OF TERMS

■ 1. 'That you'

Means the identity of the pedestrian. Under section 169 of this Act a constable may require a person committing an offence under section 37 to give his/her name and address, and if that person fails to do so s/he is guilty of an offence.

■ 2. 'being a person on foot'

Means walking or running etc as opposed to being carried in or on a vehicle or riding a horse etc. It has been held that a person on foot pushing a bicycle when using a zebra pedestrian crossing was a 'foot passenger'.

■ 3. 'where a police constable (or traffic warden) in uniform'

Means a police constable (as opposed to a cadet) or a traffic warden, both of whom must be in uniform. It has been held under the drink/driving law that the object of requiring the officer to be 'in uniform' was to ensure that the constable would be easily recognised as such by the public. A designated Community Support Officer (CSO) has the s37 powers.

■ **4. 'was engaged in the regulation of vehicular traffic on a road'** See (B)4 of Offence 12. See Glossary for 'road'.

■ **5. 'did proceed across (or along) the carriageway'**

This point means that the pedestrian tried or succeeded in walking across the carriageway, ie from footpath to footpath or along the carriageway in the same direction as the traffic flow.

■ **6. 'in contravention of a direction to stop given by the constable (or the traffic warden) in the execution of his/her duty'.**

The signal must be given clearly. See (B)7 of offence 12. 'Execution of his/her duty' means that s/he should be acting in the protection of life and property.

(C) USUAL METHODS OF PROVING THESE POINTS

■ **1. 'That you'** See (C)1 of Offence 1.

■ **2. 'being a person on foot'**

This point is proved by the officer or traffic warden stating in evidence, 'A man, I now know to be John Smith, stepped from the kerb on the south side of the road and walked towards me in contravention of my signal to him to stop etc'.

■ **3. 'where a police constable (or traffic warden) in uniform'**

This point can be proved by starting the officer's or the warden's evidence by, 'I am a police constable (or traffic warden) in such and such a police force and I was in uniform'. Usually nothing further need be proved in relation to uniform but where problems can be envisaged because an officer had no helmet or tunic on, then the general appearance of the officer could be put in evidence if required in the case of a 'not guilty' plea.

■ **4. 'was engaged in the regulation of vehicular traffic'**

This point is proved by the officer or warden stating in evidence that, 'I was engaged in the regulation of traffic to allow pedestrians to cross safely etc'.

■ **5. 'did proceed across (or along) the carriageway'**

This point is proved by the officer or warden describing what the defendant did to contravene the signal as at point 2 above.

■ **6. 'in contravention of a direction to stop given by the constable (or the traffic warden) in the execution of his/her duty'.**

The officer or warden should describe how s/he gave the necessary signal, eg, 'I raised my right arm with the palm of my hand facing the defendant. The signal was clearly visible etc ....'. The execution of duty is proved as at 4 above.

27. PARKING ON WRONG SIDE AT NIGHT

Regulation 101 Road Vehicles (Construction & Use) Regulations 1986 and section 42 Road Traffic Act 1988

(A) POINTS TO PROVE

1. That you 2. did cause (or permit) 3. a motor vehicle, namely a .... 4. to stand on a road called .... 5. between the hours of sunset and sunrise 6. otherwise than with the left or nearside of the vehicle as close as may be to the edge of the carriageway 7. without the permission of a police officer in uniform.

(B) MEANING OF TERMS

■ **1. 'That you'** Means the identity of the person causing or permitting the offence.

■ **2. 'did cause (or permit)'** Note that 'using' is not included.

■ **3. 'a motor vehicle, namely a ....** See Glossary.

■ **4. 'to stand on a road called ....**

'Stand' means, in general parlance, parked.

■ **5. 'between the hours of sunset and sunrise'**

Sunset and sunrise are to be taken at the place where the alleged offences were committed.

■ **6. 'otherwise than with the left or nearside of the vehicle as close as may be to the edge of the carriageway'.**

This phrase means what it says. Obviously a line has to be drawn somewhere. Should a driver be prosecuted for being 10cm away from the kerb, or a metre away from the kerb? The circumstances of each case must be the deciding factor as the narrower the road the more important this offence becomes.

■ 7. 'without the permission of a police officer in uniform'.

This point is self explanatory.

(C) USUAL METHODS OF PROVING THESE POINTS

■ 1. 'That you' See (C)1 of Offence 1.

■ 2. 'did cause (or permit)' See (C)2 of Offence 5.

■ 3. 'a motor vehicle, namely a ....' See Glossary.

■ 4. 'to stand on a road called ....'

See (C)4 of Offence 1 for 'road'.

'Stand' is proved by the observations of the officer concerned and although it is not necessary to prove that the vehicle had been in the offending position for a particular period of time the court may find it helpful if the officer could give evidence of it, 'The vehicle was parked on Bradford Road from 20.00 hours to 21.00 hours etc'.

■ 5. 'between the hours of sunset and sunrise'

This point is proved in accordance with local custom if it is found necessary. Some courts accept the officer's word and some refer to almanacs etc.

■ 6. 'otherwise than with the left or nearside of the vehicle as close as may be to the edge of the carriageway'.

This point is proved by showing in evidence that the vehicle was the wrong way round, ie the offside or right of the vehicle was next to the kerb or that the nearside was not as close as may be to the kerb.

■ 7. 'without the permission of a police officer in uniform'.

This is proved by asking the defendant whether s/he has such permission. A police officer cannot give him/herself such permission, see *Keene v Muncaster* (1980) 124 Sol Jo 496.

(D) SUPPORTING EVIDENCE

Note 1. The exceptions to this offence are:

(a) any motor vehicle when it is being used for fire brigade, ambulance or police purposes or for defence purposes (including civil defence) if compliance with this regulation would hinder or be likely to hinder the use of the vehicle for the purpose for which it is being used on that occasion;

(b) any motor vehicle standing on a part of a road specially set aside for the parking of vehicles, or as a stand for hackney carriages, or as a stand for public service vehicles, or as a place at which such vehicles may stop for a longer time than is necessary for the taking up and setting down of passengers where compliance with this regulation would conflict with the provisions of any order, regulations or bylaws governing the use of such part of a road for that purpose;

(c) any motor vehicle waiting to set down or pick up passengers in accordance with regulations made or directions given by the chief officer of police in regard to such setting down or picking up;

(d) any motor vehicle on any road in which vehicles are allowed to proceed in one direction only; or

(e) any motor vehicle while it is being used in connection with -
   (i) any building operation or demolition;
   (ii) the repair of any other vehicle;
   (iii) the removal of any obstruction to traffic;
   (iv) the maintenance, repair or reconstruction of any road; or
   (v) the laying, erection, alteration or repair in or near to any road of any sewer, or any main, pipe or apparatus for the supply of gas, water or electricity, of any telegraph or telephone wires, cables, posts or supports or of the apparatus of any electric transport undertaking if, in any such case, compliance with this regulation would hinder or be likely to hinder the use of the vehicle for the purpose for which it is being used on that occasion.

28. FAIL TO CONFORM TO PELICAN/ PUFFIN LIGHTS

Regulation 23, Zebra, Pelican and Puffin Pedestrian Crossing Regulations 1997 and section 25 Road Traffic Regulation Act 1984

(A) POINTS TO PROVE

1. That you 2. being the driver/rider of a vehicle, namely a .... 3. did fail to comply 4. with a vehicular light signal 5. at a Pelican/Puffin crossing on .... (give location) 6. which was displaying a red light.

(B) MEANING OF TERMS

■ 1. 'That you'

Means the identity of the person driving.

■ 2. 'being the driver/rider of a vehicle, namely a .... '

See Glossary for 'driver' and 'vehicle'. 'Rider' includes motor bikes and pedal cycles. The make and registration number of motor vehicles should be shown.

■ 3. 'did fail to comply'

Means did not stop at the 'stop line'. The stop line is a solid white line across the carriageway between 1.7 and three metres (four-and-a-half to 10 feet) before the first line of studs indicating the start of the crossing (the part where the pedestrians walk).

■ 4. 'with a vehicular light signal'

Means the red light of the light sequence.

■ 5. 'at a Pelican/Puffin crossing on ....'

'Pelican' crossings look like a set of traffic lights with a similar light sequence - except that after the red 'stop' signal, a flashing amber light allows traffic to proceed if the crossing is clear. The crossing lights are controlled by a pedestrian-operated button.
'Puffin' crossing are similar to a set of traffic lights and the light sequence is the same. They use sensors to detect anyone waiting

to cross or actually crossing and keep the lights at red until crossing is complete.

The location of the crossing should be shown.

■ **6. 'which was displaying a red light'.** The red light is mandatory and means that vehicles must stop at the 'stop line'.

(C) USUAL METHODS OF PROVING THESE POINTS

■ **1. 'That you'**

See (C)1 of Offence 1.

■ **2. 'being the driver/rider of a vehicle, namely a .... '**

See (C)2 of Offence 1 for 'driver' and Glossary for 'vehicle'. 'Vehicle' is proved by describing it in a prosecution witness' statement. Riding vehicles would be proved by witness(es) or on the admission of the rider.

■ **3. 'did cause the vehicle (or part of the vehicle)'**

Proved by witness(es)' statements showing that the vehicle did not stop at the stop line.

■ **4. 'with a vehicular light signal'**

Again, a witness, usually a police officer, would say the signal was showing a red light as the vehicle went over the stop line.

■ **5 'at a Pelican/Puffin crossing on ....'.**

The particular crossing contravened must be described accurately in a witness statement, together with its location. For example: 'I was observing the Pelican button-operated crossing on New Street outside the Town Hall entrance....'

■ **6. 'which was displaying a red light'.** As point 4 above.

(D) SUPPORTING EVIDENCE

Note 1. This offence does not require a notice of intended prosecution to be served on the driver. According to regulation 12(2) and 13(2) of these Regulations, a driver has the overall responsibility to proceed with due regard to the safety of other users of the road (subject to the direction of any police constable or traffic warden).

Note 2. Be aware of other offences associated with crossings such as:

(a) loitering on a crossing - which may apply to children 'playing' with the buttons or sensors;
(b) stopping within controlled areas;
(c) overtaking on the approach to a crossing.

29. DEFECTIVE SIDE LIGHTS (COMMITTED ANY TIME)

Regulation 23(1) Road Vehicles Lighting Regulations 1989 and section 42(1) Road Traffic Act 1988

(A) POINTS TO PROVE

1. That you 2. did use (or cause, or permit to be used) 3. on a road called .... 4. a certain vehicle namely a .... 5. the lighting equipment of which required by these Regulations to be fitted, namely .... (here specify) 6. was not clean and in good working order 7. in contravention of a statutory provision relating to obligatory lamps (or reflectors) and applicable to that vehicle, namely ....

(B) MEANING OF TERMS

■ 1. 'That you'

Means the identity of the person using the motor vehicle etc.

■ 2. 'did use (or cause or permit to be used)'

This offence can also be committed when the vehicle is stationary.

■ 3. 'on a road called ....' See Glossary.

■ 4. 'a certain vehicle, namely a ....'

See Glossary.

■ 5. 'the lighting equipment of which required by these Regulations to be fitted, namely .... (here specify)'

This point means that all the statutory provisions regarding obligatory lamps and reflectors, before the vehicle can lawfully be driven, must be complied with. The most common statutory provisions require two white lights to the front and two red lights and two reflectors to the rear.

■ 6. 'was not clean and in good working order'

This point means among other things that the lamps in question must be kept clean as mud or snow could hide the light. The bulb must be in good working order and the wiring must be good, ie free from any short circuits or bad earths which could adversely affect the lamp.

■ 7. 'in contravention of a statutory provision relating to obligatory lamps (or reflectors) and applicable to that vehicle, namely ....'

Examples of common contraventions of statutory provisions are shown at point 6 above.

(C) USUAL METHODS OF PROVING THESE POINTS

■ 1. 'That you'

See (C)1 of Offence 1.

■ 2. 'did use (or cause or permit to be used)'

See (C)2 of offence 5. For further information regarding proving 'use' in relation to construction and use offences, see (C)2 of Offence 19.

■ 3. 'on a road called ....'

See (C)4 of Offence 1.

■ 4. 'a certain vehicle, namely a ....' 'Vehicle' is proved by describing it in a prosecution witness' statement, see Glossary

■ 5. 'the lighting equipment of which required by these Regulations to be fitted, namely .... (here specify)'

This point is proved by showing whatever is specified is the lamp or reflector in question, eg, the obligatory front nearside lamp or the rear offside reflector etc.

■ 6. 'was not clean and in good working order'

The defect must be described in detail to prove this point, eg, 'Both bulbs were blown in the front obligatory lights and two white lights were not being shown to the front' or, 'The rear nearside reflector was broken and part of it was missing, leaving only about a square centimetre of reflective material' etc.

■ **7. 'in contravention of a statutory provision relating to obligatory lamps (or reflectors) and applicable to that vehicle, namely ....'** As this offence can be committed at any time the fact that it was dark at the time could be shown to assist the court in deciding on punishment.

(D) SUPPORTING EVIDENCE

The times of sunset and sunrise can be proved by reference to an almanac. Where the time is crucial to the offence the prosecution should be in a position to be able to prove the actual times in that locality from observations, should they be so required.

Note 1. This offence does not apply to –

(a) a rear fog lamp on a vehicle which is part of a combination of vehicles any part of which is not required by the Regulations to be fitted with a rear fog lamp;
(b) a rear fog lamp on a motor vehicle drawing a trailer; or
(c) a lamp, reflector or rear marking which, during daytime hours is fitted to a combat vehicle.
A 'combat vehicle' is a military vehicle used for the carriage of tanks, guns etc.

Note 2. An offence will not be committed when a defective lamp or reflector is found on a vehicle in use on a road between sunrise and sunset if such a lamp or reflector became defective during the journey which is in progress or if arrangements have been made to remedy the defect with all reasonable expedition.

Note 3. In *Payne v Harland* [1980] RTR 478, it was held that where the defective sidelight is within the headlight unit, both the sidelight and the headlight must work.

30. INTERFERENCE WITH VEHICLES

Section 9 Criminal Attempts Act 1981

(A) POINTS TO PROVE

1. That you 2. did interfere 3. with a motor vehicle (or trailer) (or with anything carried in or on a motor vehicle or trailer) 4. with the intention that a specified offence shall be committed by yourself or another.

(B) MEANING OF TERMS

■ 1. 'That you'

This means the person interfering with a motor vehicle etc.

■ 2. 'did interfere'

The dictionary definition of 'interfere' is to meddle with or come into collision with something. Therefore any meddling with a vehicle with intent to steal it or part of it etc would amount to 'interference'. Examples would include prising the hub caps off, breaking a door lock, trying to remove badges or mascots, twisting electric wires together, breaking a steering lock, etc.

The essence of this offence is to protect the vehicle before an actual theft or 'taking without the owner's consent' takes place.

■ 3. 'with a motor vehicle (or trailer) (or with anything carried in or on a motor vehicle or trailer)'

'Motor vehicle' and 'trailer' have the same meanings assigned to them as under the Road Traffic Act 1988, see Glossary.

'Anything carried in or on a motor vehicle or trailer' includes the roof rack or its contents; articles inside a vehicle such as maps, coats, bags etc; goods in vans or lorries or trailers etc.

■ 4. 'with the intention that a specified offence shall be committed by yourself or another.'

The mental element of this offence is that the 'interference' must be, in the accused's mind, for the purpose of committing a specified offence by him/herself or by another.

The specified offences are:

(a) theft of the motor vehicle or trailer, or part of it;

(b) theft of anything carried in or on the motor vehicle or trailer; and

(c) section 12(1) Theft Act 1968 (take and drive away without consent).

Note that if it is shown that the accused intended that any one of these offences should be committed, it matters not that it cannot be shown which it was.

(C) USUAL METHODS OF PROVING THESE POINTS

■ 1. 'That you'

In these days of videoed car parks, the video may help to prove the identity of the offender. Otherwise witness statements and/or the interview would be the most likely way.

■ 2. 'did interfere'

Again video evidence or the statement of a witness would provide the proof of this point. For example: 'I saw the youth smash the quarter light glass of the rear offside passenger door and put his hand through…'

■ 3. 'with a motor vehicle (or trailer) (or with anything carried in or on a motor vehicle or trailer)'

This point is normally proved by describing the make, model etc of the motor vehicle or trailer, in the police officer's or other witness statement. If the interference is with something carried in or on the motor vehicle or trailer the witness statement may read, 'I saw the man untie the straps of the trailer tarpaulin at the read of the trailer and lift up the tarpaulin. . .'

■ 4. 'with the intention that a specified offence shall be committed, by yourself or another'.

A person's 'intent' can be proved in a variety of ways. For example, either by his/her own admission; by the facts speaking for themselves (r*es ipsa loquitur*); by him/her telling a witness of his/her intentions before embarking on the crime; or by other circumstantial evidence such as the accused needing spare parts for his/her 'hot hatch' and the one s/he is interfering with happens to be the same model and colour etc.

The best and strongest evidence would be admissions during the interview that the accused intended, for example, to steal the car to break it up for parts; to take it without consent for a joy ride; or to steal the mobile phone and sheepskin jacket lying on the back seat. If the accused did not intend to commit a specified offence him/herself but was interfering with the motor vehicle to enable a more 'skilled' person to 'hot wire' the car, then this would be proved in their respective interviews.

(D) SUPPORTING EVIDENCE

Note 1. This offence fits between 'going equipped' and 'taking a vehicle without the owner's consent. The offence can be committed anywhere.

Note 2. Other connected offences include:

(a) 'tampering with a motor vehicle' but this offence is restricted to a road or local authority parking place where the person gets on the vehicle or tampers with the brake or other part of its mechanism (section 25 Road Traffic Act 1988);

(b) 'going equipped for stealing' (section 25 Theft Act 1968) see offence 18 - taking a conveyance is included in 'theft';

(c) 'taking a conveyance without the owners' consent, or knowing it has been so taken, or drives or allows himself/herself to be carried in or on it' (s12(1) Theft Act 1968) see Offence 11.

(d) Also consider section 22A Road Traffic Act 1988 causing danger to road users *inter alia* (among other things) interfering with a motor vehicle, trailer or cycle .

31. MOBILE PHONE USE WHILE DRIVING

Regulation 110(1) Road Vehicles (Construction and Use) Regulations 1986 and section 41D Road Traffic Act 1988

(A) POINTS TO PROVE

1. That you 2. did use (or cause, or permit to be used) 3. on a road called .... 4. a motor vehicle, namely ...... 5. when you were using 6. a hand-held mobile telephone.

(B) MEANING OF TERMS

■ **1. 'That you'**

means the person using the motor vehicle.

■ **2. 'did use (or cause or permit to be used)'** See Glossary.

■ **3. 'on a road called ....'** See Glossary.

■ **4. 'a motor vehicle, namely ....'** See Glossary.

■ **5. 'when you were using'**

means the dictionary definition of 'using' – application to a purpose, to employ. All 'uses' of a mobile phone would suffice eg phoning, reading, texting, checking phone numbers, pictures, calendars, emailing etc. Any other 'interactive communication function (ICF)' is included and is defined as 'sending or receiving oral/written messages, facsimile documents of still or moving images and using the internet'.

■ **6. 'a hand-held mobile telephone'**

means held in the hand at some point during the 'use' of the phone ie receiving or making a call or performing any other ICF. Mobile telephone is not defined but the normal usage of the phrase should not cause any problem if it is one of the many types in current use. The phone needs to be able to be carried around ie mobile, and capable of telephone communication. Where the device is not a telephone Reg 110(4) includes a device other than a two-way radio, which performs an ICF by transmitting and receiving data. A two-way radio, means wireless telegraphy apparatus operating on recognised frequencies such as those used by emergency services.

(C} USUAL METHODS OF PROVING THESE POINTS

■ **1. 'That you'** See (C}1 of offence 1.

■ 2. 'did use (or cause or permit to be used)'
See (C}2 of offence 5 and 19.

■ 3. 'on a road called ....' See (C}4 of offence 1.

■ 4. 'a motor vehicle, namely ....' See Glossary.

■ 5. 'when you were using'
is proved by a witness seeing the use or an admission by the user. Where there is a denial further evidence of telephone records showing time and date of calls/texts are important. General seizure of mobile phones for evidence is debatable but for serious offences there is the common law power per *Ghani v Jones* [1969] 3 All ER 1700. See (D) *post*.

■ 6. 'a hand-held mobile telephone'
is proved as the last point was, from witness' observations. In cases of doubt the make, type, serial numbers, service provider etc. should be recorded for follow up enquiries regarding its ICF. See (D) *post* for exemptions.

(D) SUPPORTING EVIDENCE

Note 1. In *Ghani v Jones* 1969 ante, it was held that seizure is permitted if :

i. reasonable grounds to believe serious crime committed and that the person in possession of the article had committed the crime or implicated in it;
ii reasonable grounds to believe that article was the fruit of crime, or used to commit the crime;
iii. not kept longer than reasonably necessary; and,
iv. lawfulness judged at the time, not on what happened later.

Note 2. Exemptions are two-way radios under Reg 110(4) and under Reg 110(5) when:

(a) calling emergency services on 112 and 999;
(b) responding to genuine emergency, and
(c) unsafe/impracticable to stop driving.

Note 3. Bear in mind the further offence of supervising a learner driver and using a mobile phone.

Section 2

Crime

1. WASTING POLICE TIME

Section 5(2) Criminal Law Act 1967 offender

(A) POINTS TO PROVE

1. That you 2. did cause wasteful employment of the police 3. by knowingly making a false report to .... (specify person, not necessarily a constable) 4. (a) tending to show that an offence had been committed; or (b) to give rise to apprehension for the safety of any person (or property); (c) to show that you had information material to a police inquiry.

(B) MEANING OF TERMS

■ 1. 'That you'

Means the identity of the person committing the offence.

■ 2. 'did cause wasteful employment of the police'

Means that the offender actually caused police time to be wasted in one of the three ways listed at point 4, ie falsely reporting a possible offence, danger to a person(s) or property or that the reporter had material information.

■ 3. 'by knowingly making a false report to ....'

This point shows that guilty knowledge must be present. The offence is not 'making a false report', but 'knowingly making a false report'. The person to whom the report was made should also be named to help to establish guilt.

■ 4.(a) 'tending to show that an offence had been committed, or'

This point includes conduct such as a straightforward report of a false crime to anyone, but it will usually be made to a constable, eg that a person's car has been stolen or taken without authority or that a house has been burgled.

■ 4. (b) 'to give rise to apprehension for the safety of any person (or property) or'

False reports that a person is missing from home or that a bomb is in a building (which is more likely to be encountered in practice) come under this point. Note the offence of making a bomb hoax call etc, under section 51(2) Criminal Law Act 1977. There is no requirement for the Director of Public Prosecutions' consent for section 51.

■ **4. (c) 'to show that you had information material to a police inquiry'.** This point includes a person who falsely reports that s/he knows who is responsible for a particular crime or where stolen property etc, is hidden. It is difficult to pinpoint any one category of persons likely to commit this offence as a variety of motives will be involved.

(C) USUAL METHODS OF PROVING THESE POINTS

■ 1. 'That you'

The identity of the offender can be proved by the person who took the false report stating who s/he took it from. Problems might arise when the false report is made via a telephone. In such cases the witness can try to identify the voice, but the best evidence is an admission by the offender that s/he was the caller.

■ 2. 'did cause wasteful employment of the police'

The police should be in a position to prove how many hours are actually wasted. The hours can be calculated by totalling all the man hours expended as a result of the false report, eg a false report is made by a driver involved in a hit and run accident that his/her car had been stolen and at the time of the accident was driven by the thief and not himself. If two constables spent 10 hours each investigating the false report before discovering the truth then the total hours wasted would be 20.

■ 3. 'by knowingly making a false report to .... (Specify person, not necessarily a constable)'

This point has to be proved and in common with other offences where 'what a person knows' has to be proved, difficulties can arise. A judge has said that the state of a person's mind is as much a fact as the state of his/her digestion. But unless the defendant admits s/he knew the report to be false the prosecution will have to rely on circumstantial evidence. The easiest way to prove this point is to ask a question like 'Did you know the report you made to .... (person's name) was false?' and if the answer is 'Yes' then this would be good evidence.

Circumstantial evidence could take the form of showing the defendant wished to cover up an offence committed by himself, such as driving over the prescribed limit, being involved in an accident and then, as mentioned at (C) 2 ante, alleging that someone else was driving at the time of the accident. The report need not be made to a constable. A false report of theft could be made to a next-door neighbour, perhaps to cover up for dealing with property wrongfully, and then the neighbour could make a genuine report to the police about the false theft, thereby causing police time to be wasted. The neighbour would not be liable for this offence, but the person who made the false report could probably be prosecuted.

■ 4. (a) 'tending to show that an offence had been committed, or'

This point can be proved by what was said in the report. The person who took the report should include the exact words or writing of the report in his/her evidence and show that the report tended towards showing an offence had been committed.

■ 4. (b) and (c).

These points can be proved as in point 4(a) above, with the end result being suitably altered.

(D) SUPPORTING EVIDENCE

This offence cannot be proceeded with except by or with the consent of the Director of Public Prosecutions (DPP). Such consent helps to provide uniformity among police forces when considering prosecuting for an offence which can be committed in so many different ways and for so many different reasons. Note that the DPP's consent is not required where a penalty notice for disorder is issued.

2A. FEAR OR PROVOCATION OF VIOLENCE

Section 4(1) Public Order Act 1986

(See Racial Aggravation Chart at Offence 2E.)

(A) POINTS TO PROVE

1. That you 2. did at .... 3. use towards another person 4. threatening or abusive or insulting words or behaviour or distribute or display to another person any writing, sign or other visible representation, namely ...., which is threatening abusive or insulting, 5. with intent to cause that person to believe that immediate unlawful violence would be used against him/her or another by a person, or 6. to provoke the immediate use of unlawful violence by that person or another or 7. whereby that person is likely to believe that such violence would be used or it is likely that such violence would be provoked.

(B) MEANING OF TERMS

■ **1. 'That you'** Means the identity of the offender.

■ **2. 'did at ....'**

The place where the offence was committed should be inserted here. Section 4(2) of the Public Order Act 1986 extends the old section 5 breach of the peace offence by providing: 'An offence under this section may be committed in a public or a private place, except that no offence is committed where the words or behaviour are used, or the writing, sign or other visible representation is distributed or displayed, by a person inside a dwelling and the other person is also inside that or another dwelling'. 'Dwelling' means any structure or part of a structure occupied as a person's home or as other living accommodation (whether the occupation is separate or shared with others) but does not include any part not so occupied, and for this purpose 'structure' includes a tent, caravan, vehicle, vessel or other temporary or movable structure (section 8).

■ 3. 'use towards another person'

This phrase means that the threats etc, must be towards another person. In other words, no offence would be committed if another(s) was (or were) not present who could be abused, insulted or threatened etc. In *Atkin v DPP* (1989) 153 JP 383 it was held that the words 'uses towards another person' mean that threatening words must be addressed directly to another person who is present and either in earshot or aimed at as being putatively in earshot.

It is inappropriate to use the words 'another person' in an information charging an offence under section 4 Public Order Act 1986 because the person having the belief that unlawful violence would be used has to be the SAME PERSON as the person threatened, abused or insulted, *Loade v DPP* (1990) 90 Cr App R 162.

■ 4. 'threatening or abusive or insulting words or behaviour or distribute or display to another person any writing, sign or other visible representation, namely .... which is threatening or abusive'

The phrases mean the same as under the old section 5 Public Order Act 1936. 'Threatening', 'abusive' or 'insulting' should be given their ordinary meanings. Words or behaviour show that the offence can be committed by using words or merely by actions or behaviour.

'Distributes or displays to another person any writing, sign or other visible representation', should all be given their ordinary meanings. This means the giving out or showing of any written matter or a sign, eg sandwich board, or other visible representation which would threaten, abuse or insult another person.

In practice it is more common to find the words or behaviour part of the offence being breached rather than the distributing or displaying part.

The whole phrase under this point only creates one offence and section 7(2) of the 1986 Act provides that for the purposes of the rules against charging more than one offence in the same count or information, each of sections 1 to 5 create one offence. Therefore, it would be correct to charge 'using threatening and insulting words and behaviour ....'.

The mental element or *mens rea* of the offender for this point is as follows: section 6(3) provides that a person is guilty of an offence under section 4 only if s/he intends his/her words or behaviour, or the writing, sign or other visible representation, to be threatening or abusive, or is aware that it may be threatening or abusive. This means that the offender's words, behaviour, writing, sign or visible representation must be deliberately threatening or abusive as opposed to reckless, accidental or blamelessly inadvertent.

If such intent cannot be shown, the awareness part of this mental element definition could be used. This is easier to prove and would require the subjective examination of the offender by asking questions such as, 'Would an offender of the level of his/her intelligence have been aware?'

■ 5. 'with intent to cause that person to believe that immediate unlawful violence would be used against him/her or another by any person'

This means a deliberate frame of mind on the part of the offender to cause a certain belief on the part of the victim. This is a hard part to prove and where the evidence of intent falls short, the point at 7 following, ie, 'whereby that person is likely to believe ....' could be charged or reported. Whether the victim did believe that immediate violence would be used is immaterial so long as the offender intended to cause the victim to have that belief.

'Immediate unlawful violence' means that circumstances involving delayed violence or lawful violence, such as a lawful rugby tackle during a game, would not amount to this offence.

'Violence' means any violent conduct, so that:

(a) except in the context of affray, it includes violent conduct towards property as well as violent conduct towards persons, and

(b) it is not restricted to conduct causing or intended to cause injury or damage but includes any other violent conduct (for example, throwing at or towards a person a missile of a kind capable of causing injury which does not hit or falls short) (section 8).

'Would be used against him/her or another by any person' means against the victim or the victim's baby, friend or spouse etc, The offender need not be the person to offer the violence as a friend of the offender would come within the phrase, 'by any person'.

■ 6. 'to provoke the immediate use of unlawful violence by that person or another'

The intent to provoke the immediate use of unlawful violence means an intention by the offender to cause the other party or another to use unlawful violence.

■ 7. 'whereby that person is likely to believe that such violence would be used or it is likely that such violence would be provoked'.

This is the easier part of the offence to prove. In the first instance where the police officer dealing with the offender cannot prove an intent, as point 5 above, s/he should consider this point.

'Likely to believe' or 'likely to be provoked' means, that in the opinion of the police officer and the court, these likelihoods might occur. Note that for this part of the offence to be proved neither likelihood need occur.

It was held in *R v Horseferry Road Metropolitan Stipendiary Magistrate, ex p Siadatan* [1991] 1 All ER 324 that the phrase 'such violence' must be 'immediate' and the phrase refers back to the words 'immediate unlawful violence.'

(C) USUAL METHODS OF PROVING THESE POINTS

■ 1. 'That you'.

This point is proved by the officer who arrests the suspect stating that the defendant in court is the person involved. Any witness could prove this point.

■ 2. 'did at ....'

The location of the offence can be described in evidence by any witness of the incident to show that it occurred in a public or a private place. Note the offence cannot be committed inside a dwelling when the other person is inside that or another dwelling.

■ 3. 'use towards another person'

This can be proved by a civilian witness or a police officer witnessing the incident and describing in his/her evidence that the threats etc, were towards the other person. There is no requirement to identify the other person but this may be advantageous in certain circumstances, eg when it is suspected that a defence may be used that there was no other person.

■ 4. 'threatening or abusive or insulting words or behaviour or distribute or display to another person any writing, sign or other visible representation, namely .... which is threatening or abusive'

The type of actions used by the offender should be explained in the witness statement(s). The actual words (if any) should be recorded, eg, 'You bastard, I'll cripple you here and now'. The mental element or mens rea under section 6(3) should be considered at this point. Good questioning is essential to prove clearly an intent or awareness on the part of the offender. For example: 'Did you intend to threaten, abuse and insult that person when you said, "You bastard, I'll cripple you here and now"? He replied, "No". I said, "Were you aware that you might threaten, abuse or insult him?" He said, "Yes".'

■ 5. 'with intent to cause that person to believe that immediate unlawful violence would be used against him/her or another by any person'

This point, if used, can be proved by the officer in the case questioning the offender, for example, 'Did you want that Notown Football Club supporter to believe that you and your friends were going to hit him?' He said, "Yes, but I wasn't going to hit him".'

■ 6. 'to provoke the immediate use of unlawful violence by that person or another'

If this point is charged or reported it may be proved by the officer in the case questioning the offender on the lines of: 'Did you intend to provoke the Notown football supporters into violence? He said, "Yes, I wanted you lads to catch them at it and arrest them".'

■ 7. 'whereby that person is likely to believe that such violence would be used or it is likely that such violence would be provoked'.

The officer dealing and/or civilian witnesses could help prove this point by including in their evidence observations, such as:

'The crowd of visiting football supporters were likely to believe they were going to be attacked', or, 'It was likely that the visiting supporters would lose their tempers and attack the home crowd'.

(D) SUPPORTING EVIDENCE

Note 1. It was held under the Public Order Act 1936 that a police officer could be the 'other' person.

Note 2. In *Winn v DPP* (1992) 156 JP 881 it was held that although section 4 creates only one offence, that offence may be committed in four different ways. Common to all four is the requirement that the accused must intend or be aware that his/her words or behaviour are or may be threatening or abusive and must be directed to another person.

Note 3. Note that the additional offence under section 31 of the Crime and Disorder Act 1998 is also committed if 'racially aggravated' (see Racial Aggravation Chart at offence 2E)

2B. CONDUCT LIKELY TO CAUSE HARASSMENT, ALARM OR DISTRESS

Section 5 Public Order Act 1986

(See Racial Aggravation Chart at Offence 2E.)

(A) POINTS TO PROVE

1. That you 2. did at ....
3. use threatening or abusive words or behaviour,
4. or disorderly behaviour, or
5. display any writing, sign or other visible representation which was threatening or abusive
6. within the hearing or sight of a person
7. likely to be caused harassment, alarm or distress.

(B) MEANING OF TERMS

■ 1. 'That you,'

Means the identity of the disorderly person.

■ 2. 'did at ....'

This point means that under section 5(2) and (3) an offence under this section may be committed in a public or private place, except that no offence is committed where the words or behaviour are used, or the writing, sign or other visible representation is displayed by a person inside a dwelling and the other person is also inside that or another dwelling.

It is a defence for the accused to prove:

(a) that s/he had no reason to believe that there was any person within hearing or sight who was likely to be caused harassment, alarm or distress; or
(b) that s/he was inside a dwelling and had no reason to believe that the words or behaviour used, or the writing, sign or other visible representation displayed, would be heard or seen by a person outside that or any other dwelling; or
(c) that his/her conduct was reasonable.

Note that 'dwelling' means any structure or part of a structure occupied as a person's home or as other living accommodation (whether the occupation is separate or shared with others) but does not include any part not so occupied, and for this purpose 'structure' includes a tent, caravan, vehicle, vessel or other temporary or movable structure.

■ 3. 'use threatening or abusive words or behaviour'

Threatening or abusive should be given their ordinary meanings. Words or behaviour show that the offence can be committed by using words or merely by actions or behaviour.

The whole phrase does not create more than one offence.

Under section 7(2) - for the purposes of the rules against charging more than one offence in the same count or information - each of sections 1 to 5 creates one offence.

The state of mind or *mens rea* required for this offence is explained in section 6(4) viz: 'A person is guilty of an offence under section 5 only if s/he intends his/her words or behaviour, or the writing, sign or other visible representation, to be threatening or abusive, or is aware that it may be threatening or abusive; or (as the case may be) s/he intends his/her behaviour to be or is aware that it may be disorderly.' Only those points (B)3, 4 and 5 of this offence are reflected in section 6(4) as per *DPP v Clarke* [1992] Crim LR 60.

Also see *Vigon v DPP* [1998] Crim LR 289 where this offence could be committed by behaviour such as peeping into changing rooms or installing a video camera for such purposes.

■ 4. 'or disorderly behaviour'

This point is not defined but it is felt that any conduct which is not orderly and is not covered by 'threatening or abusive words or behaviour' would suffice, eg kicking a dustbin down the street.

Note the defence if the accused can prove his/her conduct was reasonable. In *Percy v DPP* [2002] Crim LR 835 it was held that the defendant's conduct should be considered in relation to Article 10 of the European Convention on Human Rights (freedom of expression). The conduct in question was the defacement of the American flag (the defendant's own property) near an RAF base.

■ 5. 'displays any writing, sign or other visible representation which was threatening or abusive'

This point means showing any written matter or other visual matter such as a swastika which would threaten or abuse

■ 6. 'Within the hearing or sight of a person'

This point means that the offence must be near enough to another person(s) for it to be heard or seen. The 'person' could be a police officer who is caused harassment, alarm or distress, but taking into account all the facts the magistrates might equally decide that the words or behaviour did not have this effect, *DPP v Orum* [1988] 3 All ER 449.

Note the defence shown at point 2 above, when the offender has no reason to believe anyone was within hearing or seeing distances who was likely to be caused harassment, alarm or distress, eg if some people could see him, but they were a long way off. There is a further defence where the accused proves s/he was inside a dwelling and has no reason to believe his/her conduct would be heard or seen outside that dwelling or any other dwelling (section 5(3)). It was held in *Chappell v DPP* (1988) 89 Cr App Rep 82 that to deliver through the letter box some writing etc, does not contravene this section because the sender was not a person who 'uses... words or behaviour... within the hearing or sight of a person' who received it.

■ 7. 'likely to be caused harassment, alarm or distress'.

These terms are not defined and the ordinary meaning should be used. The point means only a likelihood of harassment etc, not an actual harassment. In *Lodge v DPP* (1988) *The Times*, 26 October it was found that it is not necessary that the person alarmed should be concerned at physical danger to himself. Alarm for the safety of an unconnected third party would suffice. Later in *Chambers and Edwards v DPP* [1995] Crim LR 896 it was held that apprehension concerning personal safety was not required for harassment to be established. Swearing at officers or in front of witnesses could amount to harassment, alarm or distress (*Harvey v DPP* [2011] QBD (Admin) 17/11/2011.

(C) USUAL METHODS OF PROVING THESE POINTS

■ **1. 'That you'** Proved by the officer who arrests the suspect stating that the defendant in court is the person involved. Any witness who saw the offence could prove this point.

■ **2. 'did at ....'**

The location of the offence can be proved by the officer in the case to show that the offender could not avail him/herself of the dwelling defence under section 5(2) and (3).

■ **3. 'use threatening or abusive words or behaviour'**

This point is best proved by taking a statement from a witness to say that s/he felt the words or behaviour were threatening or abusive. The *mens rea* or mental state of the offender must be proved to show an intent or an awareness that his/her words or behaviour were threatening or abusive. This could be done by questions and answers such as, 'Did you intend?' or, 'Were you aware etc?'

■ **4. 'or disorderly behaviour'**

This point can be proved by a description in the police officer's statement of evidence such as, 'I saw the accused push into a queue of football supporters' or, 'I saw the accused jumping over flower containers in the Market Place'. If this point is charged or reported then the accused's mental state or *mens rea* should be proved, ie an intent to be or an awareness that his/her conduct may be disorderly. Again such points can best be proved by questioning the offender.

■ **5. 'displays any writing, sign or other visible representation which was threatening or abusive'**

As pointed out, this part of the offence will be rather rare. The point can be proved by describing the display which may entail seizing the articles concerned.

■ **6. 'within the hearing or sight of a person'** This can be proved by observing the reactions of passers-by or persons to whom the threats or abuse were directed, eg, 'I saw two old ladies hurry past looking disgusted and saying, "You ought to be locked up" '. Better proof would be obtained by taking statements from the 'other' person(s) to say what they saw or heard.

■ **7. 'likely to be caused harassment, alarm or distress'.** This can be proved by taking statements from an aggrieved person(s) to say how harassed, alarmed or distressed s/he was. Where this is not possible the officer dealing could show in his/her evidence that it was likely that the other party would be harassed, distressed or alarmed. It would be good evidence if witnesses said they were harassed, alarmed or distressed.

(D) SUPPORTING EVIDENCE

The word 'insulting' has been removed from this section 5 offence - by section 57 Crime and Courts Act 2013 - in the interest of free speech under the Human Rights Act - but still remains in section 4A *(post)*.

As mentioned under (D) of the previous offence (2A Fear or provocation of violence), a police officer may be threatened or abused. For the purposes of *mens rea* or the mental state of the accused - where the awareness of the accused is impaired by intoxicants - s/he shall be taken to be aware of that which s/he would have been aware if not intoxicated, unless s/he shows either that his/her intoxication was not self-induced or that it was caused solely by the taking or administration of a substance in the course of medical treatment (section 6(5)).

Note 1. In subsection (5) 'intoxication' means any intoxication, whether caused by drink, drugs or other means, or by a combination of means (section 6(6) Public Order Act 1986).

Note 2. If this offence is racially aggravated, the more serious offence under section 31 of the Crime and Disorder Act 1998 should be considered (see Racial Aggravation Chart at offence 2E).

2C. INTENTION TO CAUSE HARASSMENT, ALARM OR DISTRESS

Section 4A Public Order Act 1986

(See Racial Aggravation Chart at Offence 2E.)

(A) POINTS TO PROVE

1. That you 2. did at .... 3. with intent to cause a person harassment, alarm or distress 4. use threatening, abusive or insulting words or behaviour, or disorderly behaviour or 5. display any writing, sign or other visible representation which was threatening, abusive or insulting namely .... 6. thereby causing that or another person harassment, alarm or distress.

(B) MEANING OF TERMS

■ **1. 'That you'** Means the identity of the offender.

■ **2. 'did at ....'** Means the place where the offence was committed. See (B) 2 of the previous offence.

■ **3. 'with intent to cause a person harassment, alarm or distress '**

Means guilty knowledge or *mens rea* on the part of the offender. This offence has been designed to remedy persistent racial harassment but it applies equally to other types of harassment. In *R (on application of R) v DPP* [2006] EWHC 1375 (Admin) a 12-year-old boy was arrested for a section 4A offence for gestures/shouting obscenities at the police. It was held that 'distress' required 'real emotional disturbance or upset'.

■ **4. 'use threatening, abusive or insulting words or behaviour, or disorderly behaviour'**

See (B) 3 and 4 of the previous offence. Also in *Hammond v DPP* [2004] Crim LR851, the words 'stop immorality, homosexuality and lesbianism' were found to be insulting.

■ 5. 'display any writing, sign or other visible representation which was threatening, abusive or insulting, namely ....'

See (B) 5 of the previous offence.

■ 6. 'thereby causing that or another person harassment, alarm or distress'.

This point differs from the previous offence which only requires that the harassment etc is LIKELY to be caused. In this intentional offence the harassment etc must be shown to have been caused. Note that causing harassment etc to another person, other than the one intended to suffer harassment, would suffice for this offence.

(C) USUAL METHODS OF PROVING THESE POINTS

■ 1. 'That you'

Is proved usually by the arresting officer or other witness who saw the offending behaviour.

■ 2. 'did at ....'

The arresting officer or other witness could prove this point. The defence of being inside a dwelling should be borne in mind.

■ 3. 'with intent to cause a person harassment, alarm or distress'

The best proof of intent is from the mouth of the offender, but persistent offending or other circumstantial evidence would suffice. A question such as, 'Did you realise that swastika you displayed would cause distress?' should elicit the intent of the accused.

■ 4. 'use threatening, abusive or insulting words or behaviour, or disorderly behaviour'

See (C)3 and 4 of the previous offence (2B, Conduct likely to cause harassment, alarm or distress).

■ 5. 'display any writing, sign or other visible representation which was threatening, abusive or insulting, namely ....'

This point will be encountered less often than the previous point. Proving it may entail seizing the offending article for evidence and describing the circumstances in the appropriate witnesses statement. A phrase similar to the following will be necessary, 'I took possession of the swastika banner which was being displayed on the synagogue steps. I saw two women begin to cry when they saw the swastikas.'

■ **6. 'thereby causing that or another person harassment, alarm or distress'.**

Again, this point can be proved from the observation of the arresting officer, or better still from a witness statement made by the offended party. Bear in mind that the person whom the accused originally intended to harass etc need not be the person finally harassed. A statement from the person finally harassed would prove this point.

If this offence is racially aggravated, the more serious offence under section 31 of the Crime and Disorder Act 1998 should be considered (see Racial Aggravation Chart at offence 2E).

2D. STALKING ETC WITHOUT VIOLENCE

Sections 1 and 2 Protection from Harassment Act 1997

(See Racial Aggravation Chart at Offence 2E)

(A) POINTS TO PROVE

1. That you 2. pursued 3. a course of conduct 4. on at least two occasions 5. while knowing (or while you ought to have known) 6. that it amounted to harassment 7. of another.

(B) MEANING OF TERMS

■ **1. 'That you'** Means the identity of the offender.

■ **2. 'pursued'** The dictionary definition of pursued includes 'follow with intent to capture or kill' but it is likely that the legislators used this word to mean, 'stick to', 'aim at', 'persistently attend', 'continued' (as in continued or pursued a line of inquiry).

■ 3. 'a course of conduct'

Means the *modus operandi* (method of operation). Nuisance mail, telephone calls, emails, following, photographing etc could all be considered. 'Conduct' includes speech. However, note that there must be a 'course' of conduct, ie an onward movement or pattern of conduct.

Section 7(3A) provides that a person's conduct shall be taken, if aided, abetted, counselled, or procured by another:

(a) to be the conduct of the other (as well as the conduct of the person whose conduct it is), and

(b) to be conduct in relation to which the other's knowledge and purpose, and what s/he ought to have known, are the same as they were in relation to what was contemplated or reasonable foreseeable at the time of the aiding, abetting, counselling or procuring.

This subsection has the effect of extending the offender's 'conduct' to any aider, abettor, counsellor or procurer.

The Serious Organised Crime and Police Act 2005 (SOCPA 2005) added section 1(1A) to the Protection From Harassment Act 1997 which prohibits a course of conduct - of knowingly harassing (or which the perpetrator(s) ought to know would harass) - two or more people - with the intention of persuading ANY person - to do, or not do something - by ANY means whether or not mentioned above.

■ 4. 'on at least two occasions'

Means two or more times, 's7(3); there must be a degree of proximity, but anniversaries could count. See *Lau v DPP* [2000] Crim LR 580, DC, and *R v Patel* [2004] 169 JP93.

■ 5. 'while knowing (or while you ought to have known)'

This is the offender's *mens rea* (state of mind). It means that the offender knew and understood his/her course of conduct, or should have known and understood the course of conduct. The 'reasonable person' test may be applied here. It can be considered as obvious to the offender that his/her course of conduct amounted to harassment **if a reasonable person in possession of the same information would consider that the course of conduct amounted to harassment of the other**. Therefore the objective test of 'What would a reasonable person have thought?' may be used to determine the accused's state of mind.

■ 6. 'that it amounted to harassment'

Harassing a person includes alarming the person or causing the person distress (Section 7(2)). Some adverse effect on the victim is necessary. The offender need not intend any harm to the victim. On the contrary, infatuation or hero worship may be the motive. It is generally the unusual or unwanted behaviour of the offender that causes distress etc in the victim.

■ 7. 'of another'

Means any person other than the offender.

(C) USUAL METHODS OF PROVING THESE POINTS

■ 1. 'That you'

Identity may be proved by evidence from the victim or witness(es) who saw or heard the offender, or by the officer dealing with the offence. In circumstances in which the victim has never seen the offender, an admission from the suspect is the ideal. The absence of such evidence will necessitate the use of forensic evidence such as DNA samples, fingerprints, handwriting comparison techniques etc.

■ 2. 'pursued'

This can be proved by demonstrating the **repeated** annoyance or distress caused to the victim; or by the **pattern** of behaviour of the offender - the pattern of letters, phone calls, sightings etc.

■ 3. ' a course of conduct'

Can be proved by showing the *modus operandi* of the offender. Examples would be by taping phone calls, by videoing the offender's presence in the vicinity of the victim's home or when following the victim in the street. A specific example would be to demonstrate the offender's presence on the front row of the theatre at a particularly actor's every performance, and then pestering the actor at the stage door.

■ 4. 'on at least two occasions'

The prosecution must prove that course of conduct was pursued more than once.

■ 5. 'while knowing (or while you ought to have known)'

This *mens rea* can be proved in the officer's interview, by the offender admitting knowledge of the distress caused, or from the inference that a reasonable person would have thought the course of conduct amounted to harassment when presented with the facts.

■ 6. 'that it amounted to harassment'

Can be proved by the victim's statement, showing that s/he was in a state of mind somewhere between worry and terror due to the offender's course of conduct.

■ 7. 'of another'

Proved by identifying the victim in his/her statement and may be from an admission by the accused.

(D) SUPPORTING EVIDENCE

Note 1. Defences to this offence are available where the suspect shows that (on the balance of probabilities) the course of conduct was pursued:

- (a) for the purpose of preventing or detecting crime;
- (b) under any enactment or rule of law, or to comply with any condition or requirement imposed by any person under any enactment; or
- (c) in such a manner as to be reasonable.

Examples of the above may include the activities of private detectives or county court bailiffs etc during the course of their duties.

Note 2. Where this offence is racially aggravated, the more serious offence under section 32 of the Crime and Disorder Act 1998 is committed (see the Racial Aggravation Chart at offence 2E).

Note 3. Also consider the offence of Harassment with fear of

violence under section 4 of the Protection from Harassment Act 1997 (see Racial Aggravation Chart at offence 2E).
Note 4. Most telephone companies have police liaison officers and 'nuisance' call departments. Improved technology has made it easier to bug/intercept and trace nuisance callers, but follow your own force instructions/procedures in this sensitive area.

2E. RACIALLY OR RELIGIOUSLY AGGRAVATED OFFENCES

Crime and Disorder Act 1998

(See Racial/Religious Aggravation Chart overleaf)

(A) POINTS TO PROVE

(a) 1. At the time of committing the offence, or immediately before or after doing so 2. the offender demonstrates towards the victim of the offence 3. hostility 4. based on the victim's membership (or presumed membership) 5. of a racial or religious group; or

(b) 6. the offence is motivated (wholly or partly) by hostility towards members of a racial or religious group based on their membership of that group.

(B) MEANING OF TERMS

■ 1. At the time of committing the offence, or immediately before or after doing so

The term 'immediately' is not defined but the further in time between the hostility and the offence - either before or after - the less chance there is of 'racial or religious aggravation' being proved.

Help may be gleaned from Robbery (offence 20) which uses 'immediately before' and the offence of Robbery under previous legislation which uses 'before' and 'afterwards'.

■ 2. offender demonstrates towards the victim of the offence

'Demonstrates towards' is the *actus reus* or the guilty act and could include actions, writing, signs, visible representations or speech. 'Towards' requires the demonstration to be directed specifically at the victim rather than to be a general demonstration.

■ 3. hostility

This means unfriendly, opposition, enmity to an outright state of warfare according to the dictionary definition. Some hostility will have an obvious root in racial or religious confrontation; other types may be more subtle and harder to prove, such as attacks on economic immigrants.

■ 4. based on the victim's membership (or presumed membership)

'Membership or presumed membership' means a 'belonging' to a group. This for example may be the obvious belonging of persons of full African decent or the less obvious membership of persons of half or quarter blood relationship.

This will be for the courts to decide but the Act helps by including persons who merely associate with such groups (eg the white girlfriend of an Asian man) and also including those who the offender presumes to be a member of a group, even if the presumption is mistaken (eg an ethnic Italian who was presumed by the offender to be Asian).

■ 5. of a racial or religious group

'Racial group' means a group of persons defined by reference to race, colour, nationality (including citizenship) or ethnic or national origins. For example, Sikhs, Jews and Romany gypsies may be considered to be racial groups.

'Religious group' means a group of persons defined by reference to religious belief or lack or religious belief. Examples would include Muslims, Jews and Atheists.

Groups defined by politics or other interests than racial or religious should not come within this offence.

RACIAL/RELIGIOUS AGGRAVATION CHART

Public Order Act 1986

S 4 POA
Fear or provocation…

S 5 POA - **Likely** to cause…

S 4A POA - **Intent** to cause…

RACIALLY/RELIGIOUSLY AGGRAVATED OFFENCES

Crime and Disorder Act 1998

S 31(1) C&DA - Any of these POA Offences when **racially or religiously aggravated**

Protection from Harassment Act 1997

Ss 1 and 2 PFHA - Stalking etc without violence

S 4 PFHA - Stalking etc with fear of violence

S 32 C&DA - Either of these PFHA offences when **racially or religiously aggravated**

Offences Against the Person Act 1861 & Criminal Justice Act 1988

S 39 CJA
Common Assault

S 47 OAPA
Assault Occasioning Actual Bodily Harm

S 20 OAPA - Wounding

S 29 C&DA - Any of these OAPA offences when **racially or religiously aggravated**

Criminal Damage Act 1971

S 1(1) CDA - destroying /damage to property

S 30 C&DA - This CDA offence when **racially or religiously aggravated**

■ 6. the offence is motivated (wholly or partly) by hostility towards members of a racial or religious group based on their membership of that group.

'Motivated', in this context, is the state of mind of the offender (the *mens rea*).

In (a)1.-5. above a 'demonstration' of individual hostility is required, while as (b)6. the 'motive' is required.

Take the offence of common assault on a black person as an example. If the phrase 'black bastard' was used immediately before, during or immediately after the assault, then (b)1.-5. above would apply.

However, consider a group of persons who 'wholly or partly' hated black people and attacked a group of Asians without any obvious 'demonstration' of hostility based on race. This 'motive' or *mens rea* is a much more difficult concept to prove.

(C) USUAL METHODS OF PROVING THESE POINTS

■ 1. At the time of committing the offence, or immediately before or after doing so

This is proved by the offender admitting, or the victim or other witness(es) stating when the hostility took place. In cases which involve telephone call, emails, photographs etc, then other methods may be appropriate.

■ 2. the offender demonstrates towards the victim of the offence

'Demonstrates towards' is proved by showing the offender's actions, either physical, verbal or written. The victim's or other witness(es)' statements would include the *actus rea.*

■ 3. hostility

The particularly hostile act would be described by the offender and/or the witnesses. For example a Nazi salute to a Jew, verbal abuse of a black person or written abuse to an Asian.

■ 4. based on the victim's membership (or presumed membership)

This would be best evidenced by a description and explanation in the victim's statement.

For example 'My parents are both Asian Indians and I am Indian in appearance. At the time of the offence, I was wearing Indian dress (give description) and a turban which is associated with being a Sikh… etc.' This could be backed by witness(es)'s description plus the observations of the officer in the case.

In cases in which the offender has rightly or wrongly **assumed** membership, then the outward manifestations could be proved by witnesses, or the inward belief during the course of the interview/taped interview/statement under caution etc with the defendant.

Where 'association' with a racial or religious group is a necessary point to prove, then statements from the person associating, and from a member of the group associated with, would be required.

For example, 'I have all white Scottish ancestry and have been the girlfriend of Ramjit Singh, an ethnic Asian, for four years'; plus 'I am the sister of Ramjit Singh and have known Christine for four years as she has visited our house most weeks over this period of time.'

■ 5. of a racial or religious group

Proof of race, colour, nationality (including citizenship), or ethnic or national origins or religion could be by a statement from the victim, or from an embassy or consul official, passport details etc, or from a religious leader if necessary.

No doubt case law will develop the definition of 'racial or religious group' and officers should keep themselves aware of additions to, or deletions from, the group. (Membership of a group by association and mistaken presumption of membership by the offender are as described above at point 4.)

■ 6. the offence is motivated (wholly or partly) by hostility towards members of a racial or religious group based on their membership of that group.

This is part (b) of the two part offence. Part (a) 1.-5. requires demonstrated hostility to the victim, and this part (b)6 requires motivation by hostility towards a racial or religious group.

It is considered that the majority of circumstances would fall into the easier to prove (a)1.-5.

However, if it in necessary to prove (b)6. then the problems of proving a state of mind are encountered. Best evidence would be an outright admission by the accused that s/he was motivated (wholly or partly) by hostility towards the racial/religious group. This could form part of a comment after being cautioned, part of a taped interview or part of a statement under caution.

Failing such an admission, then circumstantial evidence may suffice. Examples would be evidence of what the accused had said to close friends or relatives, the accused's actions, evidence of similar facts, previous conduct or conduct *post* the offence. Note that members of the Police Service are protected under this Act.

(D) SUPPORTING EVIDENCE

Note the offence of **'Hatred against persons on religious grounds'**. As from 1 October 2007 the Racial and Religious Hatred Act 2006 added to the Public Order Act 1986 section 29A to 29N.

'Religious hatred' (s29A): in this Part 'religious hatred' means hatred against a group of persons defined by reference to religious belief or lack of religious belief.

'Acts intended to stir up religious hatred' (s29B) use of words or behaviour or display of written material. A person who uses threatening words or behaviour, or displays any written material which is threatening, is guilty of an offence if he/she intends thereby to stir up religious hatred.

The Attorney General's consent is needed to charge this offence, therefore early consultation with the CPS is essential when considering such a case.

BUILDING GOOD RACE RELATIONS

A proactive check-list for constables
based on the Macpherson Report recommendations

- Know the Ministerial Priority for all the Police Service: 'To increase trust and confidence in policing among minority ethnic communities' (recommendation 1).
- Know the definition of 'racist incident': 'A racist incident is any incident which is perceived to be racist by the victim or any other person' (recommendation 12).

  Note that the subjective perception of the definition depends on what is in the mind of the victim or any other person.

  Their perception can be established from comments such as: 'I felt the graffiti to be racist as it said, "Go home", and although my parents and I were born in England, our colour attracts such comments', from the victim; OR 'I felt sorry for my neighbours as such racist graffiti must upset them even though their family has lived in England for 40 years', from 'any other person'.

  Once an incident is classed as 'racist' then records and prioritisation can take place.
- Know your force's key performance indicators to help implement, monitor and assess the Ministerial Priority (recommendation 2).
- Know your force's strategy to:
  Prevent; Investigate; Record, and Prosecute
  racist incidents.
- Know what your force is doing to encourage the reporting of racist incidents (recommendation 16).
- Be aware of the numbers of racist incidents and the detection levels in your area (recommendation 15).
- Keep abreast of – multi-agency co-operation – information exchange – surveys to show levels of equal satisfaction in all ethnic groups.

- Know your family/witness/victim/liaison officers (recommendation 23).
- Take full part in any racist awareness training and cultivate your own knowledge continuously. Appreciate the value and positive aspects of cultural diversity eg food, dress, religion, family ties etc (recommendation 48).
- Know the level of complaints of racist behaviour/attitude in your force and the outcomes (recommendation 55).
- Keep your first aid training up-to-date and practise continually (not just at exam time) (recommendation 45).
- Know the position in your local schools regarding the 'promotion of cultural diversity' as a positive issue; the number of racist incidents (if any) and other school and educational initiatives in this field (recommendation 67).

Behaviours for constables to avoid

based on common sense

- Avoid racist, sexist or homophobic behaviour/attitudes in work or domestic and social life.
- Do not encourage racist humour.
- Take care not to adversely misinterpret language or body language from persons having different cultural backgrounds than your own.
- Do not be impatient towards, intolerant of or too ready to criticise ethnic minorities, or indeed anyone else.
- Do not associate yourself with racist people either in your work, your social life, or at venues you may attend such as sporting events, concerts, demonstrations etc.

Race and diversity training

Implementing the Recommendations in Diversity matters, Home office circular 50/2003, requires all forces to complete a programme of community and race relations (CRR) training for all frontline staff, including CID and police staff.

3A. INDECENT EXPOSURE

Common law

(A) POINTS TO PROVE

1. That you 2. did unlawfully, wilfully and 3. publicly expose 4. your naked person.

(B) MEANING OF TERMS

■ 1. 'That you'

Means the identity of the person exposing himself.

■ 2. 'did unlawfully, wilfully and'

This point means intentionally as opposed to accidentally and unlawfully as opposed to lawfully such as an artist's model.

■ 3. 'publicly expose'

Publicly means an exposure which can be seen by more than one person. Men and women can commit this offence and it need not be in a public place.

■ 4. 'your naked person'.

Means, in most of the reported cases, the naked penis although it may well be that exposure of the vagina would be within the mischief the offence is trying to prevent.

(C) USUAL METHODS OF PROVING THESE POINTS

■ 1. 'That you'

Proof of the identity of an accused exposing his/her person may be difficult and, without an admission, a witness is required to say that the man/woman in the court dock is the person who exposed their person.

■ 2. 'did unlawfully, wilfully and'

This point will depend on the circumstances of each case. However, if the accused has done the same act on a number of occasions, and if s/he admits s/he did it intentionally or if s/he draws attention to him/herself etc, then unlawful and wilful conduct may be proved.

■ 3. 'publicly exposes'

Proof of 'publicly' is by showing that the exposure was to more than one person. This offence can be committed in a private place, *Ford v Falcone* [1971] 2 All ER 1138.

■ 4. 'your naked person'.

Proved by witness statement(s) showing that the person was not covered.

(D) SUPPORTING EVIDENCE

Note. This offence is rarely used as it can only be tried on indictment. If the circumstances of the offence constitute a common law public nuisance the Criminal Law Act 1977 allows for trial either way.

3B EXPOSURE

Section 66 Sexual Offences Act 2003

(A) POINTS TO PROVE

1. That you 2. intentionally 3. exposed 4. your genitals 5. intending 6. that someone 7. will see them 8. and be caused alarm or distress.

(B) MEANING OF TERMS

■ 1. 'That you'

Means the identity of the person exposing him/herself.

■ 2. 'intentionally'

Means not accidentally such as males forgetting to do up the fly zip or buttons or a females skirt blowing up in the wind minus pants.

■ 3. 'exposed'

Means to show, exhibit or uncover their genitals anywhere and need not be in a public place. In the absence of any case law to the contrary it is considered that an exposure could be through glass, via mirrors, down a mobile phone picture or through closed circuit television (CCTV).

■ 4. 'your genitals'

means the penis or vagina (not the breasts or bottom). The penis need not be erect. 'Genitals' includes female exposure but it is normally males who commit this offence.

■ 5. 'intending'

This is the second intent required by this offence. It refers to the state of mind of the suspect regarding his/her desire that someone would see the genitals and be alarmed or distressed. This intent is what the suspect wants to happen and it is not necessary that it actually does happen.

■ 6. 'that someone'

This means anyone else other than the suspect and includes male, female, boy or girl. It need not be to more than one person.

■ 7. 'will see them'

means that the suspect intended the victim to see their genitalia. It matters not if no one actually saw the genitals as long as the suspect intended them to be seen.

■ 8. 'and be caused alarm or distress'

means the suspect intended that by seeing the genitals the victim would be alarmed or distressed. There is no definition of these words, therefore the dictionary definition should be used, eg to become agitated or make unhappy. There is no requirement that an exposed penis should be erect. A male whose only intent is to urinate would not breach this offence unless an intent to cause alarm/distress was proved. Also streakers or nudists normally have no intent to alarm or distress.

(C) USUAL METHODS OF PROVING THESE POINTS

■ 1.'That you'

is proved by admission or by a witness correctly identifying the suspect. Proving identity can be difficult and may require a video identification, an identity parade and/or forensic analysis of fluids for DNA, fingerprints, footprints etc. The eight points of Turnbull (see Glossary under 'That You') should be considered when taking any witness statement.

■ 2. 'intentionally'

The state of mind can be proved by admission or from circumstantial evidence such as a penis being erect, being shown through a bus window, in public, accompanied by actions and/or words that help prove intent. Where the defence is one of accidental exposure, evidence of similar facts could be present in some cases (see *Perkins v Jeffrey* [1915] 5KB 702. Flashers are creatures of habit and it is rare to come across a first time offender.

■ 3. 'exposed'

can be proved by admission and the victim, plus any other witness statements, stating they had a clear view of the exposed penis/vagina for whatever length of time.

■ 4. 'your genitals'

Here the victim's knowledge of what a penis or vagina looks like is important. Prove in their statements that they knew how to recognise genitalia, eg 'I'm a married woman with three children' or 'I've seen my brother's when it was stiff'. Some defences have alleged the penis was merely a finger, an enlarged infantile hernia, an extended navel etc, so careful descriptions are necessary in the witness statements. Where there is no victim admissions would be required to prove the intent.

■ 5. 'intending'

Again, the state of mind can be a problem. Admissions in 'a statement under caution' or verbally are usually the best way to secure such evidence. Circumstantial evidence showing the suspect's intent that someone should see the genitals and be alarmed or distressed could include the location, length of time and words and actions. It is not necessary to prove that what was intended, actually happened. It is the suspect's 'guilty intent' or *mens rea* that must be proved.

■ 6. 'that someone'

can be proved by showing other people were in the area and that the suspects exposure was directed towards them. Admissions as to the suspect's desire that someone would see their genitals would be best evidence, but failing that, one would have to fall back on circumstantial evidence.

■ 7. 'will see them'

as with (C)5 and 6 above, admissions and circumstantial evidence coupled with the fact that it was possible to see them would help prove this point.

■ 8. 'and be caused alarm or distress.'

As above admissions and/or circumstantial evidence would prove this point. To show someone was actually alarmed etc is a good way of proving this intent, although not essential. If the exposure was via a mobile phone picture or CCTV then if the recipient was a boyfriend/girlfriend probably no offence would be committed as there would be no intent to alarm.

(D) SUPPORTING EVIDENCE

The old offences of exposure under the Vagrancy Act and The Town Police Clauses Act have been repealed. The common law offence still exists, see Offence 3A ante.

4. TELEPHONE CALLS – OFFENSIVE ETC

Section 127 Communications Act 2003

(A) POINTS TO PROVE

1. That you 2. did send a message by means of a public electronic communication network (PECN), namely a telephone, which was grossly offensive, or 3. send a message by telephone which was of an indecent (or an obscene or a menacing) character or 4. send a message by telephone to .... (specify person)

which you knew to be false for the purpose of causing annoyance (or inconvenience or needless anxiety) to the said .... (or to ....) or
5. persistently make telephone calls without reasonable cause and for the purpose of causing annoyance (or inconvenience or needless anxiety) to ....

(B) MEANING OF TERMS

■ 1. 'That you'

Means the identity of the person making the obscene etc, calls.

■ 2. 'did send a message by means of a public electronic communication network (PECN), namely a telephone, which was grossly offensive, or'

Means the message must have gone by a PECN and must be very offensive.

'PECN' means a system for the conveyance of signals of any description through the agency of electric, magnetic, or electro magnetic energy. See section 32 of the Act for the full definition. PECN includes telephone, satellite, computer / internet, mobile and terrestrial networks, blackberry, emails, text messages, facsimile/FAX, radio and TV, including cable.

Such offensive calls are usually of a sexual nature, eg heavy breathers, and also come under point 3. However, they could be offensive in other ways, such as telling a woman that her husband was having an affair, was homosexual, or had a criminal record.

■ 3. 'did send a message by telephone which was of an indecent (or an obscene or a menacing) character or'

'Telephone' means the same public system as at the alternative point at 2 above. Indecent and obscene are usually in the form of heavy breathing, or suggestions of an obscene sexual nature etc. Menacing calls include threats of violence to the person or property.

■ 4 and 5. These points are similar to points 2 and 3 above but vary slightly in the content of the call.

For point 4, examples would include falsely telling a woman her husband was dead or that he was having an affair. Point 5 includes action such as needlessly ringing a telephone in the early hours of the morning.

(C) USUAL METHODS OF PROVING THESE POINTS

■ 1. 'That you'

When the offender is on the other end of a telephone this point is usually difficult to prove. Apart from an admission, the prosecution have to rely on catching the offender red-handed by keeping observations on a suspect or by a telephone company official tracing a persistent caller when s/he is actually making a call etc, or by the recipient having a system which displays the number of an incoming call. The recipient could also give evidence that she recognised the voice or recorded the offender.

■ 2. 'did send a message by telephone which was grossly offensive or'

As with the last point the telephone causes problems. The receiver of the call could give evidence that the grossly offensive message was received on a public telephone.

■ 3. 'send a message by telephone which was of an indecent (or an obscene or a menacing) character, or'

This point is proved as the last point with the recipient explaining the indecent, obscene or menacing nature of the call.

■ **4 & 5.** These points are proved as the last two points.

(D) SUPPORTING EVIDENCE

The recent massive increase in the use of mobile phones has led to large numbers of 'nuisance' calls. To combat this, most phone companies have appointed police liaison officers and set up nuisance calls departments. Improved technology is helping to increase detection rates and the offence of Stalking (Offence 2D) has made the investigation of nuisance calls easier. Also see Offence 6 where a telephone call could be a section 47 assault.

5. OFFENSIVE WEAPON

Section 1(1) Prevention of Crime Act 1953

(A) POINTS TO PROVE

1. That you 2. without lawful authority or reasonable excuse 3. had with you 4. in a public place called .... 5. an offensive weapon namely a ....

(B) MEANING OF TERMS

■ **1. 'That you'** Means the identity of the person who had the offensive weapon with him.

■ **2. 'without lawful authority or reasonable excuse'**

Lawful authority means the lawful carrying of the weapon such as a policeman's truncheon. The lawful carrying of something like a car jack which is used to cause injury on the spur of the moment does not necessarily make it an offensive weapon (*R v Dayle* [1973] 3 All ER 1151).

The prosecution are safer trying to show some interval of time between forming the intent to use the article to injure and the actual use. Reasonable excuse may be found where a person carries a weapon as self-protection from imminent attack (*Evans v Hughes* [1972] 3 All ER 412). Carrying a knife on the off chance of being attacked, and weapons carried by dance hall security guards have been held not to be a reasonable excuse. *Chalal v DPP* [2010] EWHC 439 (Admin) – Casual work can be a reasonable excuse for possessing a blade in public, ie a lock knife used for cutting straps off boxes at his uncle's firm.

In *R v Sundas* [2011] EWCA Crim 985 it was held that there was a need to show 'intent to cause harm' before considering 'reasonable excuse'.

■ **3. 'had with you'**

This point means that the accused must have known s/he had the weapon with him/her (R v *Cugullere* [1961] 2 All ER 343). Constructive possession, ie at his/her house or any place when the accused is not there, is not sufficient.

■ **4. 'in a public place called ....'** 'Public place' includes any highway and any other premises or place to which at the material time the public have or are permitted to have access whether on payment or otherwise (section 1(4) Prevention of Crime Act 1953). In *R v Mehmed* [1963] Crim LR 780 where the accused had an air pistol which s/he produced in another's private house, it would be reasonable to assume that s/he must have carried it in a public place to get it there or to take it away. It was open to the court to make this inference.

■ **5. 'an offensive weapon namely a ....'.**
Offensive weapon means any article **made or adapted** for use for causing injury to the person or **intended** by the person having it with him/her for such use by him/her, or by some other person, s1(4) Prevention Of Crime Act 1953 as amended by the Public Order Act 1986 Schedule 2, paragraph 2. Therefore three categories exist, ie (i) made; (ii) adapted; or (iii) intended. Examples of **'made'** include a knuckleduster or bayonet. 'Disguised knives (where the blade is hidden inside something like a belt buckle, mobile phone or a pen) and butterfly knives (where the handle swings around the blade) will be regarded as **'made'**. Flicknives are offensive weapons *per se* per *Gibson v Wales* [1983] Crim LR 113. Examples of '**adapted**' include a bottle specially broken to use as a weapon, or a belt if it has been specially studded for use as a weapon. Examples of an article **'intended'** for use as an offensive weapon include a dart which the accused intends to throw in a football crowd or a pocket full of stones which the accused intends to throw at members of a rival demonstration.

An intent to cause injury by shock is sufficient and apparently means the same as an intent to cause injury to the person (*R v Rapier* [1980] Crim LR 48). Recklessness as to causing injury is insufficient (*R v Byrne* [2004] crim LR 582.

(C) USUAL METHODS OF PROVING THESE POINTS

■ **1. 'That you'** Can be proved by the officer dealing with the case proving an admission by the accused that s/he was the person concerned. Any witness who saw the incident and could identify the accused could prove this point.

■ **2. 'without lawful authority or reasonable excuse'**

The proof of this point is on the defence and they must prove on the balance of probabilities that the accused had it with him/her with lawful authority or reasonable excuse. It is advisable for the prosecution to anticipate any such defence and try to negate any fraudulent defence at the investigation stage.

■ **3. 'had with you'** This point is proved by the police officer or other witness stating, 'He held the dart in his hand' or, 'The knuckleduster was visible sticking out of his jacket pocket', etc. The defence could always allege only a constructive possession and that there was no actual possession in the absence of a witness stating positive actual possession.

■ **4. 'in a public place called ....'**

Proof must be available that the offence occurred at a place coming within the definition at point (B)4 of this offence. Note that the court could infer that the accused had been in a public place where no such direct evidence exists. (See point (B)4, *R v Mehmed*.)

■ **5. 'an offensive weapon namely a ....'.**

Proof of an offensive weapon depends on which of the three categories, outlined at point (B)5 of this offence, is used.

If 'made' or 'adapted' is used the prosecution need only prove that the accused had it with him. They need not prove that the accused had it with him/her with the intention of using it to cause injury to the person. This proof is only required when the 'intended' category is used.

Therefore where an otherwise innocent article is concerned it can only become an offensive weapon if the accused intended to use it to cause personal injury. This can be proved by comments from the accused to the effect, 'I carried it to use in case I was ever attacked'. The case of *R v Dayle* outlined at (B)2 shows that the offence is 'had with him' and not 'picked up on the spur of the moment'. The prosecution should try to prove an interval of time between forming the intention and using the article to injure when the third category of 'intended' is used (*Ohlson v Hylton* [1975] 2 All ER 490).

(D) SUPPORTING EVIDENCE

Note the further offence under Section 1A of threatening with an offensive weapon in a public place in such a way that there is an immediate risk of serious physical harm to that other person. Note 2. From 18.08.2016, section 141 Criminal Justice Act 1988 includes 'Zombie knives' and bans their sale, manufacture, rental or importation.

6. ASSAULT OCCASIONING ACTUAL BODILY HARM (AOABH)

Section 47 Offences Against the Person Act 1861

(A) POINTS TO PROVE

1. That you 2. did assault .... (specify person)
3. thereby occasioning him/her actual bodily harm.

(B) MEANING OF TERMS

■ **1. 'That you'** Means the identity of the accused.

■ **2. 'did assault .... (specify person)'**

Assault means any intentional or reckless act which causes a person to apprehend immediate unlawful force or personal violence.

■ **3. 'thereby occasioning him/her actual bodily harm'.**

Means a hurt or injury which is more serious than a common assault and less serious than an unlawful wounding chargeable under section 20 Offences against the Person Act 1861 (permanent disability or disfigurement). Examples of actual bodily harm include lost teeth, extensive bruising, minor fractures, loss of consciousness.

An assault causing a psychiatric or nervous condition is also sufficient (*R v Miller* [1954] 2 QB 282), as are strange telephone calls if they make the victim apprehensive and cause psychological damage (*R v Ireland* [1997] 161 JP 569 HL). Where pain is alleged as a result of a non-physical assault the court must have psychiatric evidence of whether the conduct could have caused the injury. *R v Morris* [1998] Cr App Rep 386. See *R (on the application of T) v DPP* [2003] Crim LR 622, for loss of consciousness coming within 'actual bodily harm'.

The assault must occasion the bodily harm.

(C) USUAL METHODS OF PROVING THESE POINTS

■ **1. 'That you'** The identity of the accused can be proved by the evidence of the victim or an admission etc.

■ **2. 'did assault ....'**

'Assault' is proved by showing the accused's actions come within the definition of assault at (B)2 of this offence. In most cases there will be physical contact between the accused and victim and this can be proved by any person who witnessed the offence.

Where an assault cannot be proved, an offence of unlawful wounding or inflicting grievous bodily harm contrary to section 20 of the Offences against the Person Act 1861 can be considered. Where the injury is very minor then common assault under section 39 Criminal Justice Act 1988 should be considered. See offence 6A.

■ **3. 'thereby occasioning him/her actual bodily harm'.**

This point is proved by describing the injury sustained by the victim, eg, 'He had several bruises about 4cm in diameter on his face'. Photographic and/or medical evidence could be considered if it is thought that the injuries would be difficult to prove. The statement made by the victim should also contain a description of the injury. Any medical examination report by a police surgeon or the victim's own doctor etc may be required. The prosecution is not obliged to prove that the defendant intended to cause actual bodily harm or was reckless as to whether such harm would be caused (*R v Savage* and *DPP v Parmenter* [1991] 3 WLR 914).

(D) SUPPORTING EVIDENCE

Section 29 of the Crime and Disorder Act 1998 gives a higher penalty if racially or religiously aggravated. Therefore it would greatly assist the court if the motive was shown in the evidence.

6A COMMON ASSAULT

Contrary to section 39 Criminal Justice Act 1988

(A) POINTS TO PROVE

1. That you 2. did assault by beating or 3. intentionally or recklessly caused .... (enter name of person assaulted) to fear that s/he would be immediately subjected to 4. unlawful violence.

(B) MEANING OF TERMS

■ **1. 'That you'**

Means the identity of the person who assaulted the victim.

■ **2. 'did assault by beating'**

Means that an injury was inflicted on the victim, but note that a section 39 offence should only be charged if the injury was trivial, eg grazes or scratches, otherwise a section 47 Offences against the Person Act 1861 offence (assault occasioning actual bodily harm) should be charged (see offence 6).

This example deals with the beating side, but there are two distinct offences, assault by threats, and assault by beating. See *DPP v Taylor, DPP v Little* [1992] i All ER 299.

■ **3. 'intentionally or recklessly cause .... to fear that s/he would be immediately subjected to**

Means that the victim feared the violence would occur right then, therefore the accused must have been physically in a position to use violence against the victim.

■ **4. 'unlawful violence'**

Means that the accused was not acting lawfully, eg prevention of crime, effecting arrest or lawful chastisement of a child by a parent or someone acting in *loco parentis*.

(C) USUAL METHODS OF PROVING THESE POINTS

■ 1. 'That you'

This is proved by the victim or witnesses to the assault and by questioning the suspect.

■ 2. 'did assault'

Witness statements and the interview evidence should cover the definition of assault by battery as at (B) above. For example: 'I saw a man I know to be Peter Shepherd hit my husband on his nose with the clenched fist of his right hand….' 'I saw his nose was red and swollen.'

■ 3. intentionally or recklessly caused .... (enter name of person assaulted) to fear that s/he would be immediately subjected to

Witnesses would explain the behaviour which made the victim fear that an assault was about to be made upon him.

■ 4. 'unlawful violence'

This can by proved by showing that the accused had no right in law to assault the victim (see defences in (D) below).

(D) SUPPORTING EVIDENCE

Note 1. Certain defences are available to this offence; if raised it is for the prosecution to counter them.

'Consent' is such a defence, eg a blow struck in a game of rugby, if not likely or intended to cause bodily harm, would usually be lawful as the participants give their tacit consent to the rough and tumble of the game, but extreme behaviour would not be deemed to have received consent.

'Moderate correction' may be a defence for chastising a child but see section 58 Children's Act 2004.

'Justification' for an assault may be claimed when done in self-defence, as a response to provocation during the resistance of violence in defence of someone else or in defence of property etc.

Note 2. Section 76 of the Criminal Justice and Immigration Act 2008 refreshes the defence of 'self-defence'. The defence will apply where there was an – honest belief – of the necessity to use force and – the degree of force was not disproportionate – to the circumstances as he/she believed them to be. The Court must recognise the difficulty of using proportionate force on the spur of the moment. It should honour the defendant's honest view of the facts even when such a belief was mistaken. This would not apply if the mistaken belief was induced by voluntary intoxication.

7. ASSAULT ON POLICE

Section 89(1) Police Act 1996

(A) POINTS TO PROVE

1. That you 2. did assault .... (specify officer), a constable of the .... Police Force (or Constabulary) 3. in the execution of his/her duty.

(B) MEANING OF TERMS

■ 1. 'That you'

Means the identity of the person who assaulted a constable.

■ 2. 'did assault .... (specify officer), a constable of the .... Police Force (or Constabulary)'

Assault means an act which intentionally or recklessly causes another person to apprehend immediate and unlawful personal violence (*Fagan v Metropolitan Police Commissioner* [1968] 3 All ER 445).

■ 3. 'in the execution of his/her duty'

Means duties connected with protecting life and property, preventing and detecting crime and keeping the peace. The constable must not be exceeding his/her authority, such as detaining a person where s/he has no power of arrest. S/he must not act unlawfully in other ways such as remaining on premises after being lawfully requested to leave. There is much case law on this point. In a recent case a Custody Sergeant was held to be in the execution of his duty when he removed an obstructive or abusive person from the custody suite using reasonable force (*R (on the application of Bucher) v DPP* [2003] 167 JPN 182).

(C) USUAL METHODS OF PROVING THESE POINTS

■ **1. 'That you'** Can be proved by the officer who has been assaulted giving evidence of identification.

■ **2. 'did assault .... (specify officer) a constable of the .... Police Force (or Constabulary)'**

Assault must be proved in accordance with the definition at point (B)2 of this offence. In most cases the accused will strike the officer who should describe the assault in detail. Photographs can be considered in cases where problems are foreseen.

■ **3. 'in the execution of his/her duty'.**

Can be proved by describing the duty being performed, eg, 'I said to John Brown "You are being arrested for conduct likely to cause a breach of the peace and offend public decency" and was about to hold his arm and caution him when he struck me in the face with his left fist etc'.

If there is any doubt about being able to prove this point successfully the prosecution should consider other offences.

Where any actual bodily harm is occasioned section 47 of the Offences against the Person Act 1861 may be appropriate (see offence 6 ante). Sections 18 and 20 of the same Act can also be considered where there is a wounding or grievous bodily harm, with or without intent.

(D) SUPPORTING EVIDENCE

Note 1. Also be aware of the offence of assaulting a person assisting a constable.

Note 2. In *Metcalf v CPS* [2015] EWHC 1091 (Admin) an unlawful push by an officer made no difference to a charge of wilful obstruction. That being the case, it may be reasonable to presume the same view would be taken if the charge was assaulting an officer.

8. OBSTRUCTING POLICE

Section 89(2) Police Act 1996

(A) POINTS TO PROVE

1. That you 2. did wilfully obstruct (or resist) .... a constable of the .... Police Force (or Constabulary) 3. acting in the execution of his/her duty.

(B) MEANING OF TERMS

■ 1. 'That you'

Means the identity of the person obstructing the police.

■ 2. 'did wilfully obstruct (or resist) .... a constable of the .... Police Force (or Constabulary)'

Wilful obstruction means a deliberate, intentional act which makes it more difficult for the police officer to carry out his/her duty. Examples include warning someone so as to render police investigation fruitless (*Hinchcliffe v Sheldon* [1955] 1 WLR 1207) and drinking alcohol after driving to frustrate the breath test procedure (*Ingleton v Dibble* [1972] 1 QB 480).

■ 3. 'acting in the execution of his/her duty'.

See (B)3 of Offence 7.

(C) USUAL METHODS OF PROVING THESE POINTS

■ 1. 'That you'

The officer obstructed should give evidence to identify the accused.

■ 2. 'did wilfully obstruct (or resist) .... a constable of the .... Police Force (or Constabulary)'

This point can be proved by the officer concerned describing the obstruction in detail, for example, 'I saw John Jones signal to several car drivers to reduce their speed before passing the police operated speed check' etc. Care should be taken by the prosecution to show the obstruction was deliberate and intentional to negate any defence of accident or mistake.

■ 3. 'acting in the execution of his/her duty'.

See (C)3 of Offence 7.

(D) SUPPORTING EVIDENCE

Note 1. Also be aware of the offence of obstructing someone assisting a constable.
See Note 2 of Offence 7. Assault on Police.

9. SEXUAL ASSAULT

Section 3(1) Sexual Offences Act 2003

(A) POINTS TO PROVE

1. That you 2. did intentionally 3. touch 4. sexually 5. another person 6.without that person's consent and did not reasonably believe that person consented.

(B) MEANING OF TERMS

■ **1. 'That you'** The identity of the person carrying out the sexual assault, who can be male or female.

■ **2. 'did intentionally'**

A person's intentions can be difficult to prove. The *'mens rea'* or what is in the mind of the suspect is as much a fact as what is in the stomach of the offender. 'Intentionally' means deliberately as opposed to 'accidentally'.

■ **3. 'touch'**

The term 'assault' in the repealed offence of 'indecent assault' has been replaced by 'touch' which it is hoped will simplify this area. In the absence of any case law, 'touching' will cover all physical contact. It should include touching not only with the hand, but any other part of the body and with any instrument or article. Touching through anything should suffice eg where a man rubs his groin against a woman in a queue for sexual purposes even though it is through layers of clothing. Where there is 'penetration' of the vagina, anus or mouth, the more serious offences should be considered although there will always be the less serious offence of sexual assault committed. See (D) 'Supporting Evidence' to this Offence.

■ 4. 'sexually' Under section 78 of the SOA 2003 where a 'reasonable person' would consider that:

(a) whatever the circumstances or any persons purpose in relation to it, it is, because of its nature, sexual; or
(b) because of its nature, it may be sexual and, because of the circumstances or the purpose of any person in relation to it (or both), it is sexual.

Examples of (a) would include overtly sexual acts like grabbing another's genitals or playing with a female's breasts or bottom. Examples of (b) would include the less obvious like a kiss or a hand on a females thigh accompanied by indecent suggestions etc (circumstances/purpose).

In *R v H* [2005] EWCA Crim 732 a man said to the victim 'Do you fancy a shag?' and grabbed her track suit bottoms in the pocket area. He tried to put his hand over her mouth. It was held that this was a 'sexual touching' because:

(1) The jury had answered 'Yes' to 'Was the touching sexual because of its nature and surrounding circumstances?' AND
(2) Because of the circumstances/purpose, the jury was convinced the touching was sexual.

■ 5. 'another person'

This means the victim, ie the one being sexually assaulted. It includes male or female.

■ 6. 'without that person's consent and did not reasonably believe that person consented'

This point means that the victim did not want, allow or agree to the touching or was mistaken as to their identity. It also means that the suspect did NOT reasonably believe the victim had consented. Section 74 of the Act states that a person consents if they agree by choice and if they have the freedom and capacity to make that choice. Section 3(2) provides that 'whether a belief is reasonable is to be determined having regard to all the circumstances, including any steps the suspect has taken to ascertain whether the victim consented'.

Section 75(1) provides that if it is proved:

(a) that the defendant did the relevant act;

(b) that any of the circumstances described in section 75(2) existed (see below), and

(c) that the defendant knew that the circumstances existed;

the complainant is to be taken not to have consented to the relevant act unless sufficient evidence is found to raise the issue of whether the person consented, and the defendant is to be taken not to have reasonably believed that the complainant consented unless sufficient evidence is found to raise the issue as to whether s/he or she reasonably believed it. (This is a rebuttable presumption.)

The 'circumstances' required by section 75(1)(b) above are:

(a) that any person was, at the time of the act or immediately before it began, using **violence** against the complainant, or causing the complainant to fear that immediate violence would be used against them, eg punches or threats to kill;

(b) that any person was, at the time of the act or immediately before it began, causing the complainant to fear that violence was being used, or that immediate violence would be used against **another person**, eg their child;

(c) that the complainant was, and the defendant was not, **unlawfully detained** at the time of the act, eg kidnapped, but not both in a police cell;

(d) that the complainant was **asleep**, or otherwise unconscious, at the time of the relevant act, eg in a diabetic coma;

(e) that because of the complainant's physical **disability**, the complainant would not at the time have been able to communicate to the defendant whether they consented, eg could not talk, and

(f) that any person had administered, or caused the complainant to take without their consent, a substance that, having regard to when it was administered or taken, was capable or causing or enabling the complainant to be **stupefied** or overpowered at the time of the act, eg excess alcohol (section 75(2)).

Then Section 76 provides that it is to be conclusively presumed that the complainant did not consent to the act and that the defendant did not believe the complainant consented to the act if it is proved that the accused did the relevant act and the defendant:

(a) intentionally deceived the complainant as to the nature of the act; or
(b) intentionally induced the complainant to consent to the act by impersonating a person known personally to the complainant.

This is known as an irrebuttable presumption and examples include, at (a) 'this will improve your singing voice' and at (b) the victim's husband, but not a celebrity who is not known personally to the victim.

(C) USUAL METHODS OF PROVING THESE POINTS

■ 1. 'That you'

This point is proved by admission and/or the victim giving evidence of identification. Such evidence as hairs, saliva and seminal fluid for DNA tests, finger prints and foot prints etc and video or identification parades identification would all help. Although corroboration is not required in law it may be wise to look for such evidence in practice, even for the suspects identity, see *R v Midwinter* (1971) 55 Cr App R 523. Also see the eight points of Turnbull at p6 ante.

■ 2. 'did intentionally'

Sometimes the facts will speak for themselves (*res ipsa loquitur*) as when a man forces a woman to masturbate him.

Conversely the so-called accidental touching of a woman's breasts on the Underground trains would be difficult to prove. Evidence of similar facts could be considered to negate the defence of accident or to prove the intent. The suspect's desire to obtain sexual pleasure should be explored at interview, eg 'did this turn you on?' 'did you get sexual feelings from touching her?' 'did you get an erection?' 'did you cum?' etc.

Intentions are best proved from the suspect's admissions, preferably under caution. Behaviour such as telling the victim not to tell anyone or covering up his/her tracks/identity may help to establish the 'intent'.

■ 3. 'touch'

This is proved from admissions from the suspect, in the victim's statement or in an independent witness' statement. Denials of touching may be refuted by forensic of fibres, fingerprints, DNA etc. The necessity of proving an 'assault' as in the old offence of indecent assault is now replaced by 'touching'.

■ 4. 'sexually'

As outlined in B4 (*ante*) the section 78 'reasonable person' test is applied to prove this point. In most cases the facts will speak for themselves, ie most sexual assaults will be overtly sexual under section 78(a) and will be proved in the victim's and /or witness' statements. The boarderline cases such as a kiss would need to be proved sexual under section 78(b) ie the circumstances and /or the suspect's purpose would be considered sexual by a reasonable person.

The interview is important in the absence of overtly sexual acts, eg 'why did you place the baby sitter's hand on your knee while you were kissing?' 'do you think a reasonable person would consider this to be sexual?'.

■ 5. 'another person'

This point is proved by identifying the victim in his/her statement, eg 'I am Joan Doe, I am 17 years' old and attend Sometown School for Girls... etc.'

■ 6. 'without that person's consent and did not reasonably believe that person consented'

'Without consent' can be proved in the victim's statement or from other witness statements and from any circumstantial evidence. It must be proved that the victim hadn't the choice to refuse and hadn't the freedom or the capacity to refuse (section 74). This may involve medical evidence.

Proving the suspect did not reasonably BELIEVE the victim consented may be difficult. This is another part of the *mens rea* in this offence, ie the guilty state of mind. This can be proved from an admission by the suspect.

Section 3(2) assists by providing that whether a belief is reasonable is to be determined from all the circumstances, including any steps the suspect took to ascertain whether the victim consented. 'All the circumstances' will be proved from any interview with the suspect and the witness statements. 'Any steps taken' will also be proved in a similar fashion, eg 'Did you ask her or anyone else if she had learning difficulties or special needs?' 'Did you ask her or anyone else if she understood what you were doing?'.

Proving the rebuttable presumption under section 75(1)&(2) and the irrebuttable presumption under section 76(1)&(2) should be done via the suspect's interview and witness statements. Medical / forensic evidence may be necessary in some cases.

(D) SUPPORTING EVIDENCE

Sexual Assault is an offence which is often committed in private and it is often word against word. Corroboration is not called for in law but a stronger case would be made out if such evidence was found.

Penetration by force of the vagina or anus with any other part of the body or another object could be charged as 'assault by penetration' (Section 2 SOA 2003).

British subjects can commit this offence abroad if against a person under 18 years. See Schedule 2 for more offences and section 72 of the Sexual Offences Act 2003 which became law on 14th July 2008.

Note that voluntary intoxication is no defence to sexual assault (*R v Heard* [2007] EWCA Crim 125).

10. SOLICITING FOR PROSTITUTION

Section 1 Street Offences Act 1959 as amended by The Policing and Crime Act 2009

(A) POINTS TO PROVE

1. That you, aged 18 or over, 2. persistently 3. did loiter (or solicit) 4. in a street (or public place) called .... 5. for the purpose of prostitution.

(B) MEANING OF TERMS

■ **1. 'That you, aged 18 or over'** Means the identity of the person (male or female) loitering or soliciting – who must be 18 years or over (Serious Crime Act 2015).

■ **2. 'persistently'**

'Persistently' means if the loitering or soliciting takes place on two or more occasions in any period of three months.

■ **3. 'did loiter (or solicit)'**

'Loiter' means passing frequently at a slow speed (*Williamson v Wright* 1924 SLT 363).

'Solicit' means to invite, entice, appeal to, or request, another person. An advertisement or notice board is not soliciting as the presence of the prostitute is required (*Burge v Director of Public Prosecutions* [1962] 1 All ER 666 and *Weisz v Monahan* [1962] 1 All ER 694).

A person who is in a street or public place can be solicited by a prostitute who is on a balcony or at a window (*Smith v Hughes* [1960] 2 All ER 859).

■ **4. 'in a street (or public place) called ....'**

'Street' is defined at section 1(4) Street Offences Act 1959 as any bridge, road, lane, footway, subway, square, court, alley or passage, whether a thoroughfare or not, which is for the time being open to the public, and the doorways and entrances of premises abutting on a street and any ground adjoining and open to a street, shall form part of the street.

'Public place' is not defined in the Act but is under the Public Order Act, *viz* 'any highway and any place to which, at the material time, the public has access, on payment or otherwise, as of right or by virtue of expressed or implied permission' which in the absence of any pertinent case law is a guideline.

■ 5. 'for the purpose of prostitution'.

Means that loitering or soliciting must be for the purpose of offering her/his body etc, for reward. Prostitution is not confined to sexual intercourse. A woman who offers her body commonly for any lewd act for reward is a prostitute. This includes a woman who merely masturbates her clients *(R v Webb [1964] 1 QB 357.*

(C) USUAL METHODS OF PROVING THESE POINTS

■ 1. 'That you, aged 18 or over'

This point of identity can be proved by the police officer who arrested (or occasionally reports) the prostitute, identifying her/him to the court. Age can be proved by birth certificate, by admission or, if necessary, by statement from someone present at the birth.

■ 2. 'persistently'

Proof of this point must be available to negate any defence of accident or mistake, eg that 'I was waiting for my boy friend or a taxi etc'. The proof usually takes the form of quoting previous convictions, cautions and other relevant antecedent history to the court, in circumstances where s/he denies on oath being a prostitute.

Before being charged with loitering or soliciting etc, the police should first caution the person (man or woman) on two occasions for loitering or soliciting etc. The caution should be entered in the appropriate register of cautions. A detailed description of the person and all other means of identifying her/him in the future should be noted as prostitutes frequently change their names and appearances.

The officer(s) who actually cautioned the person may be required to prove such caution(s) to the court.

■ 3. 'did loiter (or solicit)'

Two police officers will keep observations for prostitutes and to prove this point their evidence should contain words to the effect that, 'the accused walked slowly up and down High Street five times, stopping and talking to several men. As a result of what one of the men (the witness) John Smith said to me, I spoke to the accused' etc. Here the prostitute both loiters and eventually solicits when s/he speaks to a client. Proof of soliciting is the actual conversational meeting with a prospective client. Usually, in practice, only one of the charges is preferred, ie loitering (over a period of time) or soliciting (usually a verbal invitation).

■ 4. 'in a street (or public place)'

This point is proved by naming the street and, in nine times out of 10, will cause no problems. But in cases of doubt the definition at point (B)4 should be consulted and the particular place proved by describing how the place comes within the definition or becomes 'public'.

■ 5. 'for the purpose of prostitution'.

This point must be carefully proved to eliminate any risk of charging an innocent person who was merely asking the way or for a light etc. Good evidence would consist of an incriminating statement taken from a prospective client or an offer to do 'business' with a plain-clothed police officer.

(D) SUPPORTING EVIDENCE

Also see Home Office Circulars 006/2010 re prostitution and 008/2015 re children and prostitution.

10A. SOLICITING A PROSTITUTE

Section 51A Sexual Offences Act 2003

(A) POINTS TO PROVE

1. That you 2. solicited another person 3. for the purpose of obtaining their sexual services as a prostitute 4. in a street or public place, namely...............

(B) MEANING OF TERMS

■ 1. 'That you'

Means the identity of the person 'soliciting' a prostitute.

■ 2. 'solicited another person'

This offence requires actual 'soliciting', ie an enticing or invitation. There must be a physical act or words amounting to solicitation (*Darroch v DPP* [1990] Crim LR 814). Repeated driving along the same street is not sufficient.

■ 3. 'for the purpose of obtaining their sexual services as a prostitute'

This point means that the reason for 'soliciting' must be for obtaining 'sex' in some form from a prostitute.

'Sexual services' includes masturbation, sado masochism, oral sex and all the various practices used for sexual gratification. 'Prostitute' is defined as a person who, on at least one occasion and whether or not compelled to do so, offers or provides sexual services to another person in return of payment or promise of payment. The payment or promise of payment may be to the person offering or providing the sexual services, or to a third party (eg the pimp or boss). Whether the prostitution is due to coercion or choice makes no difference.

■ 4. 'in a street or public place, namely...........'.

This has the same meaning as in Offence 10 (B)4 *ante*. In a street or public place includes being in a vehicle.

(C) USUAL METHODS OF PROVING THESE POINTS

■ 1. 'That you'

This can be proved in a statement or admission from the suspect or from a witness statement.

■ 2. 'solicited another person'

A statement from the person solicited or other witness(es) to prove an invitation/enticement/request etc is necessary. For example, for the suspect to say to the person solicited: 'Are you doing business?' or 'How much do you charge?'

■ 3. 'for the purpose of obtaining their sexual services as a prostitute'

The actions or speech of the suspect would help prove this point. This is the *mens rea* of the offence or the 'state of mind' or 'intent' of the suspect. Evidence of asking for sex in any manner of ways would help to prove intent or purpose.

Consider questions to the suspect such as: 'Did you know this was a Red Light district?' 'Why did you come to this area?' 'What did you say to that woman?' 'It is alleged you said, "How much for a wank?". Is that correct?'

■ 4. 'in a street or public place.'

This is proved by the officer or other witness(es) naming the street or describing the public place to show that it comes within the definition. As this point includes 'being in a vehicle' the vehicle should be described in the witness statement(s). This could be backed up by questioning in the accused's police interview, eg: 'What vehicle were you in?' 'Did you open a door or talk through an open window?' 'How did you invite him/her into your car?' etc.

(D) SUPPORTING EVIDENCE

Note that this offence replaced the repealed Kerb Crawling offences (s1 Sexual Offences Act 1985) and is a much broader offence, not requiring the proof of 'persistency', or the causing of annoyance or nuisance to others.

11. TAKING CONVEYANCE WITHOUT AUTHORITY

Section 12(1) Theft Act 1968

(A) POINTS TO PROVE

1. That you 2. did, without having the consent of the owner or other lawful authority, 3. take a certain conveyance, namely a .... 4. for your own use (or for the use of ....).

(B) MEANING OF TERMS

■ 1. 'That you'

Means the identity of the person taking the conveyance.

■ 2. 'did, without having the consent of the owner or other lawful authority'

Means that this offence is not committed if the accused believed that s/he had lawful authority to do it or that s/he would have had the owner's consent if the owner knew of his/her doing it and the circumstances of it. In practice this defence is not often put forward. 'Other lawful authority' includes such things as the police moving a vehicle causing an obstruction.

'Owner' includes a person possessing the conveyance as a result of a hiring agreement or a hire-purchase agreement.

■ 3. 'take a certain conveyance, namely a ....'

'Take' means some movement of the conveyance intending to put the conveyance into motion (*Blayney v Knight* [1975] Crim LR 237). 'Conveyance' means any conveyance construed or adapted for the carriage of a person or persons whether by land, water or air, except that it does not include a conveyance constructed or adapted for use only under the control of a person not carried in or on it, and 'drive' shall be construed accordingly. As the essence of this offence is stealing a ride, handcarts and pedestrian-controlled vehicles etc, are not conveyances as they are designed for use only under the control of a person not carried in or on it. Pedal cycles are not included under section 12(1) but are specially dealt with under section 12(5).

■ 4. 'for your own use (or for the use of ....)'.

Means that a 'use' must be obtained. For example where the handbrake of a motor car is released and the car is allowed to run down a hill by itself the offence under section 12 would not be committed as it was not for his/her or another's use.

(C) USUAL METHODS OF PROVING THESE POINTS

■ 1. 'That you'

Is normally proved by the officer who saw the defendant driving etc, or another witness who can swear the defendant was driving etc, or by the defendant's admission. In *R v Vaid* [2015] EWCA Crim 298, DNA evidence from an airbag was held to prove who was the driver.

■ 2. 'did without having the consent of the owner or other lawful authority'

When the complainant's statement is obtained it should include the point that the person concerned had not got his/her (the owner's) consent to take the conveyance.

■ 3. 'take a certain conveyance namely a ....'

In the majority of cases the conveyance will be a motor car and the 'taking' is proved by a witness stating that s/he saw the defendant take the car, or by an admission to that effect by the defendant. Only the slightest movement need be proved but in practice the car will probably have travelled several miles.

'Conveyance' can be proved by describing the thing concerned and in cases of difficulty by showing that it comes within the definition of a conveyance as shown as (B)(3) of this offence.

■ 4. 'for your own use (or for the use of ....)'.

The normal 'use' is to go for a joyride, to get home after missing the last bus or train or for use in crime. The fact that it was used for his/her or another's use could be established by questions and answers between the police and the defendant.

(D) SUPPORTING EVIDENCE

Note 1. A consent obtained by a false statement as to the destination or the purpose of the journey is still valid (*R v Peart* [1970] 2 All ER 823).

Note 2. The second half of section 12(1) deals with a person who, knowing that a conveyance has been taken without authority, drives it or allows him/herself to be carried in or on it.

Note 3. See also offence 30, interference with a motor vehicle or trailers or with anything carried in or on a motor vehicle or trailer (section 9 Criminal Attempts Act 1981).

Note 4. Also consider 'aggravated vehicle-taking' section 12A Theft Act 1968 (as inserted by the Aggravated Vehicle-Taking Act 1992) viz:

'Commits an offence contrary to section 12(1) above re a mechanically propelled vehicle, and at any time after the taking:

(a) the vehicle is driven dangerously on a road/public place;

(b) an 'injury accident' occurred owing to the driving of the vehicle;

(c) a 'damage or property accident' occurs owing to the driving of that vehicle;

(d) damage is caused to the taken vehicle (including damage caused by the defendant trying to escape from the vehicle' (*Dawes v DPP* [1994] RTR 209)).

Aggravated vehicle-taking attracts an increased penalty. Defences include that the damage/accident/driving took place before the taking or when the defendant was not in or on, or in the immediate vicinity of, the taken vehicle.

12. BURGLARY – COMMITTING THEFT HAVING ENTERED

Section 9(1) (b) Theft Act 1968

(A) POINTS TO PROVE

1. That you 2. did, having entered 3. a certain building

(or part of a certain building) namely ....
4. as a trespasser 5. did steal therein (specify) ....

(B) MEANING OF TERMS

■ 1. 'That you'

Means the identity of the burglar.

■ 2. 'did, having entered'

Means that an effective and substantial entry has been made (*R v Collins* [1972] 2 All ER 1105). An entry can be made by any part of the accused's body or by an instrument held by the accused to intimidate someone in the building or to remove goods from the building. An entry cannot be made by an instrument used to make an entry such as a key or piece of wire used to pull back internal bolts. It is submitted that whether or not an entry has been made is a question of fact for the jury to decide.

■ 3. 'a certain building (or part of a certain building) namely .....'

'Building' means a substantial, permanent structure, usually constructed of brick, stone or wood, or any combination of them, which has walls and a roof. Again, this issue is one of fact for the jury, not one of law. Inhabited vehicles or vessels are included, eg houseboats or caravans, even if the inhabitant is not there (section 9(3) Theft Act 1968).

'Part of a building' will include entering a building lawfully but then going into a part of the building as a trespasser, such as entering the private quarters in a public house which was entered lawfully in the first instance or going behind an unattended counter in a shop.

■ 4. 'as a trespasser'

Means an intentional entry, whether reckless or negligent, into a building which is in possession of another who does not consent to the entry. The accused must know s/he is a trespasser or be reckless to that fact. Bogus officials, who gain entry fraudulently, would still be trespassers.

■ 5. 'did steal therein (specify) ....'.
Means steal anything contrary to sections 1 to 6, Theft Act 1968, see Offence 13.

(C) USUAL METHODS OF PROVING THESE POINTS

■ 1. 'That you'
Apart from being caught in the act, when the burglar may be identified by the witness concerned, forensic evidence sometimes helps to prove identity. Fingerprints, fibres of clothing, footprints or gloveprints etc, could be used where appropriate.

■ 2. 'did, having entered'
In the majority of burglaries this point should not be difficult to prove and a line in a witness statement to the effect, 'I saw James Stewart enter the house', would suffice.

In the case of instruments, proof of the accused's intent when entering the building with the instrument would be required, ie was the instrument only used to gain entry (no entry) or was it used to intimidate or to steal goods (when there would be an entry)?

■ 3. 'a certain building (or part of a certain building) namely .....'
A description of the building concerned in a witness statement would be sufficient proof of this point. Generally burglaries involve dwelling houses, warehouses, schools, shops etc.

■ 4. 'as a trespasser'
A sentence in the complainant's statement such as, 'This is my house and James had no right or authority to enter', is normally sufficient.

■ 5. 'did steal therein (specify) ....'. A theft must be proved. (See Offence 13 of this section for such advice.)

(D) SUPPORTING EVIDENCE

Note 1. Attempt to steal can also be charged, as can inflicting or attempting to inflict grievous bodily harm (GBH) on any person therein.

Note 2. The offence at section 9(1)(a) Theft Act 1968 can be charged where a person enters a building or part of a building as a trespasser with intent to commit theft, GBH, or unlawful damage. Note 3. Aggravated burglary can be charged when a s9 burglary has been committed and the accused has with him/her any firearm, imitation firearm, any weapon of offence or any explosive. This offence carries life imprisonment (section 10).

13. THEFT

Sections 1 to 7 Theft Act 1968

(A) POINTS TO PROVE

1. That you 2. did steal .... (specify property) of the value of .... 3. the property of ....

(B) MEANING OF TERMS

■ 1. 'That you'

Means the identity of the person who stole the property.

■ 2. 'did steal .... (specify property) of the value of ....'

'Steal' means (i) dishonestly (ii) appropriates (iii) property (iv) belonging to another (v) with the intention of permanently depriving the other of it.

(i) 'Dishonestly' generally means without a claim of right made in good faith. It will not be dishonest where the accused believes s/he had a right in law to the property or that s/he would have had the other's consent to take the property, or where s/he believes the owner could not be discovered by taking reasonable steps.

(ii) 'Appropriates' means any assumption of the rights of an owner and includes coming by property without stealing it but later assuming the rights of ownership. For example, a boy under 10 years, the age of criminal responsibility, took his friend's bicycle home and gave it to his father. Although the father came by the bicycle innocently, if he assumes the rights of an owner by selling it, for instance, he will steal it.

(iii) 'Property' - what is stolen must come within the definition of property viz: money and all other property, real or personal, including things in action and other intangible property. There are exceptions to this definition concerning land, mushrooms, wild plants and wild creatures, (unless reduced into possession).

(iv) 'Belonging to another' means belonging to someone having possession or control of the property. Possession includes a constructive possession as well as actual possession. A person can have possession or control of property without knowing of its existence (*R v Woodman* [1974] 2 All ER 955). Bags left outside a charity shop or in its bins are 'belonging to another' and taking them is theft (*R (on the application of Ricketts) v Basildon Magistrates Court* [2010] EWHC 2358 (Admin).

(v) 'With the intention of permanently depriving the other of it' briefly means treating the property as his/her own regardless of the other's rights, eg giving the property away, selling it or painting it, etc. An intent to deprive temporarily is not sufficient.

■ **3. 'the property of ....'.** Means as point 2(iv) above, the person having possession or control of the property,

(C) USUAL METHODS OF PROVING THESE POINTS

■ **1. 'That you'** Is usually proved by someone witnessing the theft, but can be proved by fingerprints, an admission by the accused, being found in possession of the stolen property, and by the use of a variety of technical aids such as a concealed camera.

■ **2. 'did steal ....'** Proof of the five parts of stealing will be dealt with as follows: (i) dishonestly (ii) appropriates (iii) property (iv) belonging to another (v) with the intention of permanently depriving the other of it.

(i) 'Dishonestly' is proved by the person to whom the property belonged stating that, 'No person had any right or authority to take the property'.

(ii) 'Appropriates' is generally proved by a witness stating that the accused picked the property up or put it in a shopping bag or a pocket. If the accused was not seen to take the property such evidence as him/her being seen near the scene of the crime or being found in possession of the property is useful. As appropriates involves assuming the rights of an owner the interview between the police officer in the case and the accused can be important. It can help to show his/her motive or state of mind if carefully worded questions are put to the accused.

In shoplifting for example CCTV evidence should be seized when possible, even if the camera was said to be pointing in the wrong direction. Include in your statement the person's name who controls the CCTV. The defence usually raise this point if not seized and could say such evidence would have exonerated their client.

(iii) 'Property' is proved in most cases by describing it in the statement of the person to whom it belongs or in the police officer's statement. In most cases it will be personal, or in other words movable, property.

(iv) 'Belonging to another' is proved by showing that the property was appropriated from someone having possession or control of it, eg the owner or tenant etc, of a dwelling house would have possession and control of all the personal property in the house, and the owner or driver of a car would have possession or control of the contents of the car. A sentence in the loser's statement to the effect that, 'the last time I saw my watch was when I put it in my locker at work' or, 'I placed my purse in my shopping basket' shows that s/he had possession or control of the property,

(v) 'With the intention of permanently depriving the other of it'. In order to prove this intent it must be shown that the accused meant to treat the property as his/her own.

In practice the following examples would indicate this intent:

(a) a shoplifter placing goods in his/her pocket or shopping bag where wire baskets are provided. It is more conclusive to allow the shoplifter to pass through any checkout without paying;
(b) a burglar leaving premises with property;
(c) a car thief who alters registration plates or the colour; or
(d) a pickpocket running off with the victim's wallet;
(e) a council tenant had removed council doors and replaced them with his own - it was held that he had treated the council doors as his own regardless of the council's rights (*DPP v Lavender* [1994] Crim LR 297).

The accused's intentions are best proved from any admission he makes when interviewed by the police.

■ **3. 'the property of ....'.** This point is proved as at 2(iv) above.

(D) SUPPORTING EVIDENCE

Where a person is found in possession of recently stolen property it can be presumed by the court that s/he stole it, in the absence of a satisfactory explanation.

14. FRAUD BY FALSE REPRESENTATION

Section 2 Fraud Act 2006

(A) POINTS TO PROVE

1. That you 2. did dishonestly 3. make a false representation 4. intending 5. to make a gain for yourself (or another), or to cause a loss to another, or to expose another to the risk of loss.

(B) MEANING OF TERMS

■ **1. 'That you'**

Means the identity of the defendant.

■ **2. 'did dishonestly'**

'Did dishonestly' means that by the ordinary standards of reasonable and honest people the behaviour would be regarded as dishonest AND that the defendant was aware that the conduct was dishonest and would be regarded as dishonest by reasonable and honest people. This is the two question test established in *R v Ghosh* [1982] QB 1053.

■ 3. 'make a false representation'

A representation is false where it is untrue or misleading AND the maker knows that it is, or might be, untrue. This is the 'guilty act' for the offence or the *actus reus*. An example would be where the defendant falsely claimed to have missed the last bus and asked for money for a taxi.

'Representation' may be any representation as to fact or law or the state of mind of the maker or another. A representation may be express or implied. Examples would be false claims of:

(a) **'fact'** – 'I am your newspaper delivery boy, you owe me £10.50 for last week's papers';

(b) **'law'** – 'You are liable to compensate me for breaching your contract with me';

(c) **'state of mind of maker or another'**,
– the implication when ordering a meal that there is the intention (or state of mind) to pay for it,
– or, 'Before Joe died he left me his gold watch'.

'Express' representation would be the spurious paper boy;
'Implied' representation would be the ordering of the meal.

A representation may be regarded as 'made' if it (or anything implying it) is submitted – in any form – to any system or device designed • to receive • to convey • or to respond to communications (with or without human intervention).

A representation may be by words, conduct or in writing, ie speech, action, text, fax, email etc and can be made to a person or machine (such as a vending machine, cash point, computer, parking meter etc using false coins, stolen or false cash cards, false identities etc).

Note 1. Normally the false representation will be made to a 'victim'. But the offence can still be committed where there is no victim, eg advertising counterfeit goods or goods that do not exist, on ebay or other internet auction site. The offence is complete as soon as the advertisement is sent.

Note 2. The other offences under the Fraud Act – at section 3 'fraud by failing to disclose information' and section 4 'fraud by abuse of position' – will sometimes overlap with section 2. Crown Prosecution Service advice may help to identify which offence best fits the circumstances. It may be better to charge/report more than one offence where doubt exists.

■ 4. 'intending'

This means the *mens rea* or guilty state of mind of the defendant, ie what s/he wants to do or to happen. It is a 'conduct' offence and not a 'results' offence. If the 'guilty intent' is present the result is immaterial.

■ 5. to make a gain for yourself (or another), or to cause a loss to another, or to expose another to the risk of loss.

This means a gain or loss in money/property only, whether temporary or permanent. **'Property'** includes real (land) or things in action/intangible, eg a cheque or stocks and shares etc. **'Gain'** includes keeping what one has and getting what one has not. **'Loss'** includes loosing what one has and not getting what one might. It is immaterial whether a loss or gain takes place so long as the defendant intended the same. Therefore to expose another to a possible loss is sufficient for this point.

(C) USUAL METHODS OF PROVING THESE POINTS

■ 1. 'That you'

Proving the identity of the person accused of fraud by misrepresentation. Normally the victim or the interviewing officer will be able to identify the suspect and prove it in their statements.

■ 2. 'did dishonestly'

This is proved from the suspect's actions or admissions.

The Ghosh test first question is: 'Would the defendant's behaviour be regarded as dishonest by the ordinary standards of reasonable and honest people?' For example, purporting to be the rent collector could be proved in the victims statement.

The second question to put under the Ghosh test (providing the first question was answered in the affirmative) is: 'Was the defendant **aware** that his/her conduct was dishonest and would be regarded as dishonest by reasonable and honest people?' This is the state of mind of the defendant and is sometimes difficult to prove. Normally good interview technique would allow for this to be proved during the offender's interview under caution.

The majority of cases will be straightforward but a few will cause problems, for example where the defendant claims a right to money owed to him and makes a false representation to obtain it. It is important that the Ghosh test is fully understood before commencing the interview.

■ 3. 'make a false representation'

This is proved from witness statements or from the interview. There is no limit on what can be construed as a false representation and will include ordering a meal and not paying; impersonation to obtain money; paying with a worthless cheque; using false/stolen credit cards; pirating another's copyright, secrecy/omissions when in a position of trust as when an antique dealer buys family heirlooms for a very low price; not divulging previous convictions to get cheaper insurance; rogue traders; climbing a fence to save paying to watch a match; downloading software without paying; obtaining satellite TV from unauthorised cards or decoders. All these various forms would be proved from witness observations including audio records, CCTV, seizing any article used for the fraud and admissions etc.

■ 4. 'intending'

The *mens rea* will normally be obvious from the defendant's actions but as it is 'the state of mind' it will sometimes be difficult to prove. One way to prove it will be from questions and answers during the interview or in any statement under caution made by the defendant. See Annex D of Code C of the Police and Criminal Evidence Act 1984 Codes of Practice.

■ 5. to make a gain for yourself (or another), or to cause a loss to another, or to expose another to the risk of loss.

Where the defendant has made a gain or caused loss to another or has merely exposed another to the risk of loss, all these can be proved from witness statements, interview or from any relevant documentary, audio or visual evidence etc (including information stored on computers, phones & similar devices).

15. HANDLING STOLEN GOODS

Section 22 Theft Act 1968

(A) POINTS TO PROVE

1. That you, 2. knowing (or believing)
3. certain stolen goods namely ....
to be stolen 4. did dishonestly 5. receive them.

(B) MEANING OF TERMS

■ 1. 'That you'

Means the identity of the person receiving the stolen goods.

■ 2. 'knowing (or believing)'

The prosecution must prove that the accused 'knew' or at least 'believed' that the goods were stolen at the time of receiving them.

■ 3. 'certain stolen goods namely .... to be stolen'

Means that the prosecution must prove that the goods were still stolen at the time they were received. For example, they would cease to be stolen where the goods had been discovered by the police who had taken control of them and were watching for the handler coming to collect them, or where the owner had ceased to have any right of restitution to the goods.

'Stolen goods' are defined in section 24 of the Theft Act 1968 as:

(1) The provisions of this Act relating to goods which have been stolen shall apply whether the stealing occurred in England or Wales or elsewhere, and whether it occurred before or after the commencement of this Act - provided that the stealing (if not an offence under this Act) amounted to an offence where, and at the time when, the goods were stolen - and references to stolen goods shall be construed accordingly.

(2) For purposes of these provisions, references to stolen goods shall include - in addition to the goods originally stolen and parts of them (whether in their original state or not) - (a) any other goods which directly or indirectly represent or have at any time represented the stolen goods in the hands of the thief as being the proceeds of any disposal or realisation of the whole or part of the goods stolen or of goods so representing the stolen goods; and (b) any other goods which directly or indirectly represent or have at any time represented the stolen goods in the hands of a handler of the stolen goods or any part of them as being the proceeds of any disposal or realisation of the whole or part of the stolen goods handled by him/her or of goods so representing them.

(3) But no goods shall be regarded as having continued to be stolen goods after they have been restored to the person from whom they were stolen or to other lawful possession or custody, or after that person and any other person claiming through him/her have otherwise ceased as regards those goods to have any right to restitution in respect of the theft.

(4) For purposes of the provisions of this Act relating to goods which have been stolen (including subsections (1) to (3) above) goods obtained in England or Wales or elsewhere either by blackmail or by fraud under the Fraud Act 2006 shall be regarded as stolen and 'steal', 'theft' and 'thief' shall be construed accordingly.

Note 1. The phrase 'in the hands of the thief' as used in subsection 2(a) above means in the possession or under the control of the thief, *R v Forsyth* [1997] 2 Crim App Rep 299 CA.
Note 2. 'Restored' as used in subsection (3) means taken into possession and not merely kept under observation (Attorney-General's Reference (No 1 of 1974) [1974] 2 All ER 899).

■ 4. 'did dishonestly'

'Dishonesty' is defined at (B)2(i) of Offence 13, theft.

■ 5. 'receive them'.

'Receiving' means acquiring exclusive control over the stolen goods or a joint possession with the thief or handler. There are numerous circumstances in which a person can 'handle' stolen goods but 'receiving' is the most common type. The other ways include 'undertaking or assisting in the retention, removal, disposal or realisation by or for the benefit of another or arranging to do so etc.' See charges being 'bad for duplicity' as explained in the preface.

(C) USUAL METHODS OF PROVING THESE POINTS

■ 1. 'That you'

The actual receiving will usually take place without being witnessed, therefore proving the accused's identity is usually on his/her admission and occasionally is similar to some thefts, ie proving identity by a concealed camera or photograph.

■ 2. 'knowing (or believing)

This knowledge, which is sometimes called 'guilty knowledge', is proved by the admission of the accused, by circumstantial evidence or by 'special evidence'. Circumstantial evidence could consist of altering or destroying identification marks; carefully concealing the stolen property; purchase at a lower price than the goods are worth; or failing to keep records where necessary, such as a scrap metal dealer.

Special evidence is dealt with at section 27(3) of the Theft Act 1968 as follows: Where a person is being proceeded against for handling stolen goods (but not for any offence other than handling stolen goods) then at any stage of the proceedings, if evidence has been given of his/her having or arranging to have in his/her possession the goods the subject of the charge, or of his/her undertaking or assisting in or arranging to undertake or assist in, their retention, removal, disposal or realisation, the following evidence shall be admissible for the purpose of proving that s/he knew or believed the goods to be stolen goods:

(a) evidence that s/he has had in his/her possession, or has undertaken or assisted in the retention, removal, disposal or realisation of, stolen goods from any theft taking place not earlier than 12 months before the offence charged: and
(b) (provided that seven days' notice in writing has been given to him/her of the intention to prove the conviction) evidence that s/he has within the five years preceding the date of the offence charged been convicted of theft or of handling stolen goods.

Therefore this provision allows the prosecution to bring the accused's more recent previous activities and convictions before the court.

The difficulties of proving what a person 'knows' or 'believes' also attracted common law assistance. Evidence of a thief that s/he had previously sold stolen property to the accused is admissible. Where the suspected 'handler' is found in possession of recently stolen property the court can presume that s/he stole or 'knowingly' received the goods if the accused does not provide an explanation of his/her possession or his/her explanation is unsatisfactory. It is for the prosecution to establish these facts, but they can be rebutted by the defence.

The following guidelines were given by the Court of Appeal with regard to proving 'knowing or believing' (*R v Hall* (1985) 81 Cr App Rep 260). 'Knowing' is for example when the accused is told that goods are stolen by someone with first hand knowledge, possibly the thief or burglar. 'Belief' is not quite 'knowledge' and could be said to be the state of mind of the accused who says to him/herself: 'I cannot say I know for certain that these are stolen goods, but there can be no other reasonable conclusion in the light of all the circumstances, and in the light of all that I have seen and heard.'

Where either of these states of mind can be proved then 'knowing or believing' can be established.

■ 3. 'certain stolen goods namely .... to be stolen'

This point can be proved by taking a statement from the owner of the stolen goods in which s/he states the details of the theft. The prosecution must go further than this and prove that the goods were still stolen at the time of the handling. Points should be mentioned such as, no one had taken lawful possession or control of the goods; that they had not been returned to the owner; or that the owner had not ceased to have rights of restitution to the goods AND that the goods were still stolen goods.

■ 4. 'did dishonestly'

Dishonesty can be proved by showing the handler had no claim of right to the stolen goods or that the owner had not given the accused any authority to handle the stolen goods etc.

■ 5. 'receive them'.

This point can be proved by showing the accused acquired exclusive control or a joint possession of the stolen goods. The most usual way this point is proved is to show that the accused had physical possession of the stolen goods.

(D) SUPPORTING EVIDENCE

There are many ways in which to commit this offence, eg undertakes or assists in retention, removal, disposal or realisation by or for the benefit of another, or if it is arranged to do so. As it is 'bad for duplicity' to charge more than one offence, care should be taken to identify the offence being investigated. The correct points to prove should be identified and the specific charge or information framed accordingly. See Preface for more information.

16. CRIMINAL DAMAGE

Section 1(1) Criminal Damage Act 1971

(A) POINTS TO PROVE

1. That you 2. without lawful excuse 3. destroyed (or damaged) .... (specify property) 4. belonging to .... (specify person) 5. intending to destroy or damage) such property or being reckless as to whether such property would be destroyed (or damaged).

(B) MEANING OF TERMS

■ 1. 'That you'

Means the identity of the accused.

■ 2. 'without lawful excuse'

Is defined at section 5 of the Criminal Damage Act 1971:

(1) This section applies to any offence under section 1(1) and any offence under sections 2 or 3 other than one involving a threat by the person charged to destroy or damage property in a way which s/he knows is likely to endanger the life of another or involving an intent by the person charged to use or cause or permit the use of something in his/her custody or under his/her control so to destroy or damage property.

(2) A person charged with an offence to which this section applies shall, whether or not s/he would be treated for the purposes of this Act as having a lawful excuse apart from this subsection, be treated for those purposes as having a lawful excuse:

(a) if at the time of the act or acts alleged to constitute the offence s/he believed that the person or persons whom s/he believed to be entitled to consent to the destruction of or damage to the property in question had so consented, or would have so consented to it if s/he or they had known of the destruction or damage and its circumstances; or

(b) if s/he destroyed or damaged or threatened to destroy or damage the property in question or, in the case of a charge of an offence under section 3, intended to use or cause or permit the use of something to destroy or damage it, in order to protect property belonging to him/herself or another or a right or interest in property which was or which s/he believed to be vested in him/herself or another, and at the time of the act or acts alleged to constitute the offence s/he believed -

(i) that the property, right or interest was in immediate need of protection; and

(ii) that the means of protection adopted or proposed to be adopted were or would be reasonable having regard to all the circumstances.

Note this excuse is limited to the offences under the Criminal Damage Act which do not involve danger to life. It is also worthy of note that the accused must honestly believe in his/her actions under this proviso. In *Lloyd v DPP* [1992] 1 All ER 982, it was held that a person did not have a 'lawful excuse' when he damaged a wheel clamp on his car after parking unlawfully in a private car park. For self-help from wheel clamping a lawfully parked car, see the comment at [2224] Crim LR 139.

■ 3. 'destroyed (or damaged) .... (specify property)'

'Destroyed' means that the property is totally ruined or permanently spoilt.

'Damaged' means something less permanent than destroyed, eg where property can be repaired or has only been partly damaged so as to reduce its value or usefulness.

'Property' is defined by section 10 of the Criminal Damage Act 1971 as: (1) In this Act 'property means property of a tangible nature, whether real or personal, including money and –

(a) including wild creatures which have been tamed or are ordinarily kept in captivity, and any other wild creature or their carcasses if, but only if, they have been reduced into possession which has not been lost or abandoned or are in the course of being reduced into possession; but

(b) not including mushrooms growing wild on any land or flowers, fruit or foliage of a plant growing wild on any land (but, could become 'property' if reduced into possession).

For the purposes of this subsection:

'mushroom' includes any fungus, and

'plant' includes any shrub or tree.

The main differences between this definition of property and the one in the Theft Act is that the Criminal Damage Act definition does not include intangible property, but does include land. A computer 'hacker' can be convicted of criminal damage after obtaining unauthorised entry to a computer system and making alterations impairing its proper use, *R v Whiteley* [1991] Crim LR 436. Also see the Computer Misuse Act 1990 for more offences.

■ 4. 'belonging to .... (specify person)'

'Belonging to' means briefly per section 10(2) of the Criminal Damage Act 1971, any person who has: (a) custody or control of; (b) any proprietary right or interest in; or (c) a charge on, the property in question. Generally, 'custody or control' as at (a) ante will cater for most offences of criminal damage.

■ 5. 'intending to destroy (or damage) such property or being reckless as to whether such property would be destroyed (or damaged)'.

'Intending' means an actual wish, desire or aim to do the damage that was done.

'Reckless' means having foresight of the natural and probable consequences of his/her acts or carrying out a deliberate act when closing his/her mind to the obvious risk of damage to the property. But see *R v G* [2003] 4 All ER 765 where it was held that there should be no conviction if, due to age or personal characteristics there was no genuine appreciation or foresight of the risks involved.

(C) USUAL METHODS OF PROVING THESE POINTS

■ 1. 'That you'

Is normally proved by someone witnessing the damage or admission by the accused during questioning by the police.

■ 2. 'without lawful excuse'

It is for the defendant to put forward any lawful excuse during the investigation of the suspected offence. It is then for the prosecution to disprove any lawful excuse which could provide a defence under section 5 of the Criminal Damage Act 1971 (see (B)2). Where no excuse is put forward it is usual practice to include in the victim's statement words to the effect, 'No person had any right or authority to damage the property'.

■ 3. 'destroyed (or damaged) .... (specify property)'

This point can be proved by describing the extent of the damage or destruction in the statement of the victim or some other witness. Where there is any doubt as to whether property has been destroyed (ie totally ruined) the easier charge to prove would be 'damaged', ie mere partial damage is sufficient. 'Property' is proved by describing the article concerned in one of the above statements and ensuring it falls within the definition at (B)3 of this offence. CCTV evidence should be seized when possible, even if the camera was said to be pointing in the wrong direction. Include in your statement the person's name who controls the CCTV. The defence usually raise this point if not seized and could say such evidence would have exonerated their client.

■ 4. 'belonging to .... (specify person)'

In most cases of damage this point is proved by the owner of the property stating that, 'This is my property .... etc.'

■ 5. 'intending to destroy (or damage) such property or being reckless as to whether such property would be destroyed (or damaged)'.

This point shows that the prosecution must prove that the accused had either an intention to destroy or damage etc, or was at least reckless as to whether the property was destroyed or damaged. When proving a person's intentions or foresight, section 8 of the Criminal Justice Act 1967 provides:

'A court or jury, in determining whether a person has committed an offence:

(a) shall not be bound in law to infer that s/he intended or foresaw a result of his/her actions by reason only of its being a natural and probable consequence of those actions; but
(b) shall decide whether s/he did intend or foresee that result by reference to all the evidence, drawing such inferences from the evidence as appear proper in the circumstances.'

Therefore such intent or foresight is usually proved by questions and answers to the effect, 'Did you realise that your actions would result in the damage you have caused?' Where the answer is, 'Yes' the case is straightforward. Where, 'No' is 'given, then the questioning should try to elicit that the accused was a reasonably educated person who should have realised or foreseen the consequences of his/her actions.

Note that the court will look at all the evidence available, not just what the accused says, before drawing any inferences. The Law Commission (Law Comm No 89) recommended the following test for recklessness: Did the person whose conduct is in issue foresee that his/her conduct might produce the result; AND if so, was it unreasonable for him/her to take the risk of producing it? Therefore, to prove recklessness, the prosecution may ask the accused questions like, 'Did you foresee the result of your conduct ....?' Where the answer is, 'Yes' the questioning could continue, 'If you foresaw the result why did you take the risk of producing it?' Where the answer shows that the accused's actions were 'unreasonable' then 'recklessness' will probably be proved.

(D) SUPPORTING EVIDENCE

Note 1. The charge should include the value of the damage or whether the value is unknown. This affects the mode of trial and penalty. Where a previously unknown amount is later determined, the charge should be amended accordingly. Presently the charge is for under £5,000, over £5,000 or unknown. A 'penalty notice for disorder' can be used if the damage is below £300.

17. TRESPASSING WITH A FIREARM

Section 20(2) Firearms Act 1968

(A) POINTS TO PROVE

1. That you 2. while you had a certain firearm, namely .... 3. with you 4. did enter (or were) on certain land situated at .... 5. as a trespasser and without reasonable excuse.

(B) MEANING OF TERMS

■ 1. 'That you'

Means the identity of the accused.

■ 2. 'while you had a certain firearm, namely a ....'

'Firearm' is defined at section 57(1) of the Firearms Act 1968 as: 'In this Act, the expression "firearm" means a lethal barrelled weapon of any description from which any shot, bullet or other missile can be discharged and includes:

(a) any prohibited weapon, whether it is such a lethal weapon as aforesaid or not;
(b) any component part of such a lethal or prohibited weapon;
(c) any accessory to any such weapon designed or adapted to diminish the noise or flash caused by firing the weapon;

and so much of section 1 of this Act as excludes any description of firearms from the category of firearms to which that section applies shall be construed as also excluding component parts of, and accessories to, firearms of that description.

Note that air weapon comes within the definition.

■ **3. 'with you'** This point means a close physical link with immediate control over the firearm. However, it is not necessary to prove that the accused had actually been carrying the firearm (*R v Kelt* [1977] 3 All ER 1099). Therefore where a car driver has a firearm on the passenger seat at the side of him/her it could be said to be 'with him'.

■ **4. 'did enter (or were) on certain land situated at ....'** 'Enter' or 'were on' cover the occasions when it can be proved that the accused entered land or where s/he was on the land. 'Land' includes land covered by water or in other words lakes, rivers, ponds etc.

■ **5. 'as a trespasser and without reasonable excuse'.** 'Trespasser' means that s/he had no licence or permission to enter or be on the land.

'Without reasonable excuse' means that the accused has not put forward an excuse for entering or being on the land which amounts to a reasonable excuse. Examples of excuses that the courts could accept as reasonable include: entering on land accidentally on a foggy day or night; entering to save life or property or being on land because of a mistake regarding permission or the location of the land.

(C) USUAL METHODS OF PROVING THESE POINTS

■ **1. 'That you'**

Could be proved by the witness who saw the defendant identifying him/her or on the defendant's admission.

■ **2. 'while you had a certain firearm, namely a .... '** Normally the officer's description would suffice but in cases of doubt expert evidence may be necessary. In *Grace v DPP* (1988) *Times* 9.12.88 it was held that evidence should be given to show the firearm was capable of firing, eg a witness who had seen a shot fired, or a from a member of the Firearms Department.

■ **3. 'with you'** Again, in the vast majority of cases there will be no doubt the defendant has the firearm 'with him' and the point can be proved by a witness stating that the defendant was carrying the firearm. In more difficult cases the prosecution must prove that there was a close physical link between the firearm and the defendant and that s/he had immediate control over it.

■ **4. 'did enter (or were) on certain land situated at ....'**
This point can be established by a witness describing how s/he saw the defendant enter on to land or that s/he was present on the land.
'Land' can be proved by a witness describing the land or land covered by water eg, 'I saw him in the middle of my three acre field' or, 'I saw him in the middle of my private fishing lake in an inflatable dinghy'.

■ **5. 'as a trespasser and without reasonable excuse'.**
This point can be proved by obtaining a statement from the owner or person responsible for the land in question to the effect that the defendant did not have any right or authority to enter or be on the land. Any 'reasonable excuse' put forward by the defendant which appears to be untrue or suspicious, should be tested by making enquiries to verify the truth and putting questions to the defendant, which can then be recorded in the police officer's statement of evidence.

18. GOING EQUIPPED FOR BURGLARY OR THEFT

Section 25(1) Theft Act 1968

(A) POINTS TO PROVE

1. That you 2. not being at your place of abode, namely at .... 3. had with you 4. a certain article namely a .... (briefly describe article) for use in the course of (or in connection with) burglary (or theft).

(B) MEANING OF TERMS

■ 1. 'That you'

Means the identity of the person 'going equipped'.

■ 2. 'not being at your place of abode, namely at ....'

Means being elsewhere than where s/he lived. The garage or grounds of a house would be classed as being 'place of abode'. Usually such offences are detected by searching suspect vehicles and persons late at night. Living rough in a car on a site was 'place of abode', see *R v Bundy* [1977] 2 All ER 382.

■ 3. 'had with you'

Means actually had with him/her as opposed to any constructive possession, such as keeping a set of skeleton keys some miles away from where s/he worked for the purpose of opening car doors.

■ 4. 'a certain article namely a ....'.

This point means any article which was made or adapted for use relating to 'burglary', or 'theft'. Examples include skeleton keys (made), wire coat-hanger bent to break into cars (adapted). It also means anything, even if not made or adapted, which the defendant had with him/her for use in the course of burglary etc, eg screwdriver, brace and bit, jemmy, gloves and car keys. Taking a conveyance is included in 'theft'.

(C) USUAL METHODS OF PROVING THESE POINTS

■ 1. 'That you'

Normally a police officer will detect this offence and could therefore identify the offender to the court.

■ 2. 'not being at your place of abode. namely at ....'

Proved by asking 'Where do you live' or by the suspect producing documentary evidence such as a utility bill. Witness statement(s) could be taken to show what is the correct 'place of abode'.

■ 3. 'had with you'

Can be proved by showing that the accused had the article in his/her pocket or in a bag s/he was carrying or probably even in the car s/he was driving etc.

■ 4. 'a certain article namely a ....'.

Firstly, this point is proved by describing the article in question. Secondly, if the article was made or adapted for use in committing a burglary or theft, then proof that s/he merely had such an article with him/her will be evidence that s/he had it with him/her for such a use.

Where the article is neither made or adapted for such a use then further evidence is needed to show why s/he had the article with him, eg a pedestrian stopped by a constable in a car park is found to have a large bunch of car keys with him.

The questioning may include the following: 'Where have you just come from?' 'Where are you going now?' 'What is your business in this car park?' 'Why do you need this large bunch of car keys?' 'Where did you get them all from?' etc. Depending on the answers follow-up inquiries may be necessary for verification purposes. Circumstantial evidence may be helpful and anyone who witnessed him/her trying a car door etc, could help to prove that the article, namely the bunch of keys, was for use in the course of burglary etc.

It should be remembered that when asking questions at the roadside, if the suspect has not been arrested:

(a) a caution should be given, and
(b) the suspect should be told that s/he is not under arrest and is free to leave.

The Fraud Act 2006 has deleted all reference to 'cheat' in this offence. Such offences are now covered in the offence of 'possession of articles for use in frauds' (s6 Fraud Act 2006).

19. MAKING OFF WITHOUT PAYMENT

Section 3 Theft Act 1978

(A) POINTS TO PROVE

1. That you 2. knowing that payment on the spot was required or expected 3. for ....

(enter the goods supplied or service done)
4. dishonestly 5. made off without having paid
6. with intent to avoid payment of ....
(show amount) being the amount due.

(B) MEANING OF TERMS

■ **1. 'That you'** means the person who enters the contract and 'bilks' or makes off.

■ 2. 'knowing that payment on the spot was required or expected'

'Knowing' means that the suspect was aware of the method of payment, eg at the end of a meal or after filling the petrol tank. This is the same whether someone asks for the payment (required) or the practice is for the customer to go to a cash desk to pay (expected).

'Payment on the spot' includes payment at the time of collecting goods on which work had been done (a clock repair) or a service had been provided (dry cleaning). If the 'expectation' of payment on the spot is agreed to be deferred, even by a deception, then this offence is not appropriate (see *R v Vincent* [2001] 1 WLR 1172).

■ 3. 'for .... (enter the goods supplied or service done)'

The more common goods and services involved in this offence include drinks, meals (sitdown and take away), petrol, taxi rides, public transport, haircuts etc.

■ 4. 'dishonestly'

It should be noted that the definition of 'dishonesty' under section 2 Theft Act 1968 does not apply to this offence. A general definition of 'dishonesty' was provided in *R v Ghosh* [1982] 2 All ER 689, ie the court must decide whether:

(a) what was done was dishonest according to the ordinary standards of reasonable and honest people, and
(b) if so, did the defendant himself, realise that his/her actions were, according to those standards, dishonest.

■ 5. 'makes off without having paid'

This means a departure from the 'spot' where payment is required, therefore it would be difficult to commit this offence if goods or services were delivered or provided at one's home address. The essence of the offence is someone sneaking, running or driving away.

■ 6. 'with intent to avoid payment of .... (show amount) being the amount due'.

Means that the prosecution must show a guilty mind or *mens rea.* The intent must be to permanently avoid payment.

This offence is not committed where the intent is only to defer or delay payment.

(C) USUAL METHODS OR PROVING THESE POINTS

■ 1. 'That you'

Proving the person's identity can be a problem because unless witnesses can give a good description or other identifying information, the suspect, when caught, could always deny being the person who 'bilked'. Video camera pictures may be helpful, when available, together with car registration numbers. Therefore the suspect's identity would be proved in the witness statement(s) or the police officer's statement/interview record.

■ 2. 'knowing that payment on the spot was required or expected'

The customary practice regarding payment may need explaining in a witness statement. This could be strengthened by an admission from the suspect during interview that s/he was aware of the system of payment.

■ 3. 'for .... (enter the goods supplied or service done)'

Again a witness statement as follows would suffice.

'I saw the driver of the Ford Focus saloon, registered number, ABC 123 park at the non-leaded pump number 6 and fill the petrol tank of the car. My register showed she had put 40 litres of petrol into the car's petrol tank ....'

■ 4. 'dishonestly'

The prosecution case would be strongest if both elements of 'dishonesty' could be proved.

Proving both elements would involve showing that what was done was dishonest according to the ordinary standards of reasonable and honest people, for example leaving a petrol station without paying would obviously be contrary to the behaviour of honest people; AND that the accused him/herself realised that his/her actions were dishonest by those standards, for example proved by question and answer during the interview: 'Have you used self-service petrol stations before?' 'Did you realise it was dishonest to drive off without paying?'

■ 5. 'make off without having paid'

The witness statement(s) would prove this point supplemented by any video recording of the event or the accused's admission. CCTV evidence should be seized when possible, even if the camera was said to be pointing in the wrong direction. Include in your statement the person's name who controls the CCTV. The defence usually raise this point if not seized and could say such evidence would have exonerated their client.

■ 6. 'with intent to avoid payment of .... (show amount) being the amount due'.

Proving the state of a person's mind is more difficult than proving the state of his/her stomach. Failing an outright admission that s/he intended to permanently avoid payment, then circumstantial evidence may have to be relied upon. The phrase *'res ipsa loquitur'* (the thing speaks for itself) springs to mind as 'running out' of a restaurant or 'driving off' from a petrol station, without paying, should speak for itself, as far as 'intent' is concerned. However, the prosecution should remember the onus is on them to prove the required intent.

(D) SUPPORTING EVIDENCE

This offence is not committed where the supplying of the goods or the doing of the service is contrary to law, or payment for the service is not legally enforceable, eg where a taxi driver refuses to complete a journey, thereby breaching the contract. Where a person is 'making off' and is stopped before s/he succeeds, then an attempted 'making off' could be considered.

20. ROBBERY

Section 8 Theft Act 1968

(A) POINTS TO PROVE

1. That you 2. did steal 3. and immediately before or at the time of doing so 4. and in order to do so 5. used force or put or sought to put a person in fear of being then and there subjected to force.

(B) MEANING OF TERMS

■ 1. 'That you'

Means the person who is suspected of the robbery.

■ 2. 'did steal'

Means the same as the offence of theft, see Offence 13.

■ 3. 'and immediately before or at the time of doing so'

This refers to the use of **force** or seeking to put a person in **fear**, which we will call the 'FF' factor. Where the FF factor does not exist immediately before or at the time of the theft, then robbery is not committed. Lesser offences such as theft and assault would have to be considered.

■ 4. 'and in order to do so'

This means that the use or threat of force must relate to the theft. Where the accused and victim had had a fight and as an afterthought the accused stole the victim's wallet, this would not be robbery. Likewise, where a victim pursues a thief and is assaulted in order to stop his/her pursuit, this will not amount to robbery.

■ 5. 'used force or put or sought to put a person in fear of being then and there subjected to force'.

This point means that a person has had force used on him/her or the accused has put or sought to put a person in fear of immediate force. Examples of force include snatching an ear-ring and tearing the ear in the process; snatching a handbag and spraining the victim's wrist in the process or punching a wife in order to steal the husband's briefcase.

Example of fear include the accused threatening to hit the victim unless s/he hands over his/her watch; or offering to punch a karate expert unless s/he hands over his/her wallet. This last example has been used to illustrate that as long as the accused sought to put a person in fear, it is not necessary to prove that s/he was actually put in fear.

Note that force or threat of force against the pet dog, or a car would not amount to robbery. A 'person' must be subjected to force or put or sought to be put in fear of force. In *P v DPP* [2012] EWHC 1657 (Admin) it was held that snatching a °cigarette did not have the 'force' necessary for robbery.

(C) USUAL METHODS OF PROVING THESE POINTS

■ 1. 'That you'

Will be proved from witness' statements or via the interview.

■ 2. 'did steal' This point should be proved as in the Offence of Theft, see Offence 13.

■ 3. 'and immediately before or at the time of doing so'

The 'FF' factor ('force and 'fear', see (B)3 of this offence) must be proved to exist at the time of the theft or immediately before, eg, 'The man punched me in the stomach before he took my bag' or, 'He frightened me with a knife as he took my motor bike.'

■ 4. 'and in order to do so'

Normally the FF factor will obviously relate to the theft but where any possible doubt exists, this point needs careful handling in the victim's statement and the accused's interview.

■ **5.'uses force or puts or seeks to put a person in fear of being then and there subjected to force'.**

The victim's statement, together with that of any witness, should prove any force used, eg 'The man pushed me heavily to the ground before snatching my handbag'. The problem is one where a person was not put in fear and the prosecution must prove that the accused sought to put a person in fear etc. Again witness statements will prove this point eg, 'I heard the man shout at the young man "You'll never play tennis again after I've broken your legs, if you don't give me your bloody bag"', or better still an admission from the accused.

(D) SUPPORTING EVIDENCE

Note. Other offences to consider in circumstances not amounting to robbery are blackmail, offensive weapons, firearms, assault and theft. Also assault with intent to rob and attempted robbery may be committed. Check previous convictions carefully as a previous 'serious offence' may bring mandatory life into play. In *R v Zerei* [2012] EWCA Crim 1114 it was held that a conviction for robbery was unsafe where a car had been taken by violence and abandoned shortly afterwards. The 'intent to permanently deprive' was doubtful.

21. UNLAWFUL POSSESSION OF A CONTROLLED DRUG

Section 5 Misuse of Drugs Act 1971

(A) POINTS TO PROVE

1. That you 2. did have in your possession 3. a controlled drug, namely .... (show name of drug)

(B) MEANING OF TERMS

■ **1. 'That you'**

Means the person suspected of possessing a controlled drug.

■ 2. 'did have in your possession'

The word 'possession' has been given a wider meaning than would be commonly perceived. Under section 37 of the Misuse of Drugs Act 1971, which is the interpretation section of the Act, subsection (3) provides that 'possession' shall include anything subject to the control of the accused which is in the custody of another. Eg the accused leaving drugs at his mother or girlfriend's house provided the accused maintains 'control' over the drugs.

The mental element of this offence is dealt with in section 28 which provides that lack of **knowledge** can be a defence. Therefore the prosecution must prove that the accused had knowledge of the 'possession' and that the substance was a 'controlled drug' (see *R v Lambert* [2001] 3 All ER 577).

Once proved the defendant must convince the court that he – neither knew of,

– nor suspected, – nor had reason to suspect,

the existence of some fact alleged by the prosecution. Eg, where the prosecution proves that s/he had cannabis resin in his/her hold-all and the accused proves someone put it there without his/her knowledge OR where it is proved that the substance was a class B amphetamine and the defendant convinces the court that s/he believed the tablets to be normal painkillers.

Two more defences exist which are pertinent to this offence, ie knowing or suspecting it to be a controlled drug,

(i) where the accused takes possession to prevent another from committing an offence. The proviso is that s/he should take all reasonable steps to destroy it or deliver it to a person lawfully entitled to take custody of it, as soon as possible after taking possession of it, or
(ii) taking possession for the purpose of delivering it to a person lawfully entitled to take custody of it, as soon as possible after taking possession of it.

A further defence which needs to be borne in mind is that of being authorised by regulations to possess it.

■ 3. 'a controlled drug, namely .... (show name of drug)'.
This means any substance which is specified in Part I, II or III of Schedule 2 of the Misuse of Drugs Act 1971.
Part I deals with Class A drugs - Class A includes: cocaine, diamorphine, lysergide (LSD), morphine, opium, whether raw, prepared or medicinal, pethidine.
Part II deals with Class B drugs - Class B includes: amphetamine, dihydrocodine, ethymorphine (3-ethy/morphine).
Part III deals with Class C drugs - Class C includes: alprazolam, bromazepam, cannabis and cannabis resin, cathine, diazepam.

(C) USUAL METHODS OF PROVING THESE POINTS

■ 1. 'That you'
This point is normally proved by the arresting officer identifying the suspect from a search or by questions and answers and later verification.

■ 2. 'did have in your possession'
Most offences of possessing drugs come to light as a result of a search under section 23 of the Act. Therefore a statement from the searching officer or a police surgeon after an 'intimate search' would prove this point.

An 'intimate search' is searching the body orifices, other than the mouth. Where the substance is found elsewhere than on his/her person a statement from the person who found it together with evidence to show it was under the 'control' of the accused would be necessary.

'Control' could be proved in other witness statements or during interview with the accused. Eg, a statement from the accused's aunt, 'He always told me to keep the box hidden and not to open it.'

A person who gave directions to a supplier after which s/he received a parcel of drugs through his/her letter-box, 'possesses' the drug at the time it is put through the letter-box, *R v Peaston* [1979] Crim LR 183.

It was held in *R v Strong and Berry* [1989] *The Times* 26 January, that being present in the same car as cannabis is not proof of possession *per se.* This is so even if someone had said there was cannabis in the car.

■ **3. 'a controlled drug, namely .... (show name of drug)'.** Proof of this point is generally the task of the scenes of crime officer and forensic science laboratories. Continuity is important and each stage of the suspected substance's journey from the suspect's pocket to a forensic science laboratory and back to the investigating officer should be carefully proved in witness statements. However in *R v Chatwood* [1980] 1 All ER 467, it was held that it was *prima facie* evidence of a substance being a controlled drug for an experienced drug user to admit possession of a substance which he identified as a controlled drug.

(D) SUPPORTING EVIDENCE

Note. There are many exemptions to possessing a controlled drug under the Misuse of Drugs Regulations 1985. Examples include constables, carriers, Post Office employees, Customs and Excise officers, laboratory staff etc, when acting in the course of their duties.

22. POSSESSION OF A CONTROLLED DRUG WITH INTENT TO SUPPLY

Section 5(3) Misuse of Drugs Act 1971

(A) POINTS TO PROVE

1. That you 2. did have in your possession 3. a controlled drug, namely .... [show name of drug] 4. whether lawfully or not 5. with intent to supply it to another.

(B) MEANING OF TERMS

■ **1, 2 and 3** See Offence 21, Possessing a controlled drug'.

■ 4. whether lawfully or not

Means that someone in lawful possession, such as a pharmacist or doctor, could commit this offence.

■ 5. with intent to supply it to another.

'Intent' is that 'state of mind' we have come across in previous offences. The prosecution must show a guilty state of mind or *mens rea*. It has been held to be 'an intent to supply' where a person to whom a drug had been deposited for safe keeping intended to return to the person who gave it to him/her (*R v Maginnis* [1987] AC 303).

(C) USUAL METHOD OF PROVING THESE POINTS

■ 1, 2 and 3

See methods at Offence 21, Possessing a controlled drug.

■ 4. whether lawfully or not

Whether the defendant had lawful or unlawful possession can be proved by questions and answers in the interview with the defendant. Other witness statements could prove this point if necessary. For example where a defendant remained silent an expert witness may prove lawful possession. The Special Warnings under the Criminal Justice and Public Order Act 1994, Section 36, may be given; ie on the accused's failure or refusal to account for objects, substances or marks, the court may draw such inferences as appear proper.

■ 5. with intent to supply it to another.

An outright admission by the accused is usually the best evidence, followed by circumstantial evidence from witnesses as to the intent, lifestyle and property owned etc.

There is a wealth of case law on this point, for example:

(a) Frequent visits to the defendant's house and persons carrying packets. A subsequent search of the house revealed large amounts of cash and some drugs and the occupant had not had paid employment for some years. The court held that it was contrary to common sense for the jury to be directed to ignore all these matters. The jury should by invited to look at the overall picture and draw such inferences as seem proper.

(b) The courts have stated that such issues must be reviewed on a case-by-case basis.

(c) It has been held that evidence of large amounts of money in the possession of the accused and an extravagant lifestyle - which on the face of it are derived from drug dealing - is admissible to help establish or otherwise the 'intent to supply' (*R v Morris* [1994] 159 JP1).

23. ABSTRACTING ELECTRICITY

Section 13 Theft Act 1968

(A) POINTS TO PROVE

1. That you 2. dishonestly 3. used without due authority (or dishonestly caused to be wasted or diverted)
4. any electricity.

(B) MEANING OF TERMS

■ 1. 'That you'

Means the identity of the person abstracting electricity.

■ 2. 'dishonestly'

Basically, dishonestly means abstracted without a claim of right made in good faith. See offence 13(B)2, Theft, for a fuller definition. It was found to be 'dishonest' where an officially disconnected meter had been reconnected by someone and the electricity was being used by squatters (*R v McCreadie and Tume* [1992] Crim LR 872 CA).

■ 3. 'used without due authority (or dishonestly caused to be wasted or diverted)'

'Used without due authority' means to operate electrical appliances etc after passing by the meter or using the same coin or card continuously where the meter has been damaged or tampered with or by using the 'black box', etc. The black box entails inserting probes as the supply enters the meter, thereby stopping the meter registering the correct amount of electricity used. Where someone uses football floodlights already left on, there is no offence. If the user switches the lights on him/herself the offence is committed.

'Dishonestly caused to be wasted or diverted' means, for example, unlawfully switching on electric storage heaters and lights at a place of employment to settle an old score with the owner, or running electricity to earth to flatten a battery etc.

■ 4. 'any electricity'.

This point is not defined but in the absence of judicial help it is considered that all types of electricity would be covered by this offence, ie alternating current from the national grid; privately produced electricity from a domestic generator; large standby batteries for use in case of emergencies or small car or flash light batteries. The quantity used is of no relevance to the offence only to the punishment.

(C) USUAL METHOD OF PROVING THESE POINTS

■ 1. 'That you'

On many occasions it is an electricity company employee who reports such offences. Therefore identity would be covered in his/her statement and backed up from the police interview.

■ 2.'dishonestly'

This point is proved by asking the suspect if s/he had any right or authority to abstract the electricity.

In *R v McCreadie and Tume* [1992] Crim LR 872 a disconnected meter was unlawfully reconnected. It was held that for 'dishonestly' it was sufficient to prove that the electricity was used without the authority of the electricity company, with no intention to pay. More in-depth questioning may be required for a 'wasting' or 'diverting' of electricity. In such cases the motive may help to prove a deliberate 'wasting' or 'diverting'.

■ 3. 'used without due authority (or dishonestly caused to be wasted or diverted)'

Can be proved by an explanation in the electricity company's employee's statement, as to how the electricity was abstracted. For example: 'On opening the meter cupboard I saw that a "black box" was attached to the live wires just before entering the meter which I removed and pointed out to PC Peter Frost...'.

'Dishonestly wasting' could be proved by a witness who could say, 'I am the school caretaker and the boy I know to be Matthew Lowery, who had been in the detention room, deliberately followed me around the school turning the electric heaters back on as I turned them off for the night...'.

■ 4. 'any electricity'.

Proof that electricity was present is necessary before the prosecution could prove an abstraction. Therefore the electricity company witness could say how much or estimate how much electricity had been abstracted. This point may be more difficult to prove where generators or batteries are involved.

As the quantity used is not an element of the offence, the mere proof of a light being illuminated for whatever period, would appear to be sufficient for an abstraction.

24. PASSING COUNTERFEIT NOTES AND COINS

Section 15 Forgery and Counterfeiting Act 1981

(A) POINTS TO PROVE

1. That you 2. did pass (or tender) as genuine
3. anything which is and which you knew or believed to be
4. a counterfeit of a currency note (or of a protected coin).

(B) MEANING OF TERMS

■ 1. 'That you'

Means the person passing the counterfeit money.

■ 2. 'did pass (or tender) as genuine'

Means the putting into circulation of the counterfeit money (even if it was immediately rejected as being a counterfeit).

Note that passing or tendering is not restricted to passing or tendering it as legal tender.

■ 3. 'anything which is and which s/he knew or believed to be'

For this offence to be committed the counterfeit money – must in fact be counterfeit, and - the accused must know it is counterfeit, or - s/he must believe it to be counterfeit.

■ 4. 'a counterfeit of a currency note (or of a protected coin)'.

'Counterfeit' means something that is not a currency note or a protected coin but resembles one of them (whether on one side only or on both) to such an extent that it is reasonably capable of passing for a currency note or protected coin, or if it is a currency note or protected coin which has been so altered that it is reasonably capable of passing for a currency note or protected coin of some other description.

'Currency note' means any note which has been lawfully issued in this country or the Republic of Ireland AND is or had been used as money in the country where it was issued AND is payable on demand OR any note which has been lawfully issued in a country other than those above AND is used as money in that country.

'Protected Coin' is any coin which is used as money in any country or is specified in an order made by the Treasury for the purpose of Part II of this Act (Forgery and Counterfeiting Act 1981).

(C) USUAL METHOD OF PROVING THESE POINTS

■ 1. 'That you'

This may be proved by the shopkeeper, bank cashier, bar person to whom the counterfeit money passed or was offered.

■ 2. 'did pass (or tender) as genuine'

This point can be proved by the circumstances of the passing as recorded in the witness statement(s).

■ 3. 'anything which is and which s/he knows or believes to be'

Guilty knowledge can be proved from his/her admissions or from a continued act of passing such money after being told the money is counterfeit

For example, the accused was told by the petrol station staff that a £20 note was counterfeit as identified by a machine. Nevertheless s/he tried to pay a bill at the newsagent's with a similar £20 note where s/he again was told that the note was imperfect at the watermark. Undaunted s/he paid the remaining £20 notes into his/her bank account and was again told by the bank that they were counterfeit. This evidence of passing after s/he knew or at least believed the notes were counterfeit would help to prove his/her state of mind.

■ 4. 'a counterfeit of a currency note (or of a protected coin)'.

Normally the note should be seized and forwarded to New Scotland Yard for expert examination. If counterfeit, the necessary statements to prove continuity from being passed, to being returned to the officer in the case will be needed. Forensic Science departments can also advise regarding suspect money and force instructions/guidance should be consulted.

(D) SUPPORTING EVIDENCE

Note 1. The offence under section 16 of the Act covers the circumstance of being given counterfeit money in change, for example, and then knowingly trying to pass it on or tender it as genuine.

Note 2. Where a person intends to hand in such money, there may be a defence - but not when the person cannot make up his/her or her mind as to the course of action to take (*R v Sunman* [1995] Crim LR 569).

Section 3

Miscellaneous offences

1. DOGS WORRYING LIVESTOCK

Section 1 Dogs (Protection of Livestock) Act 1953

(A) POINTS TO PROVE

1. That you 2. being the owner (or person in charge) 3. of a dog which worried 4. livestock .... (specify) 5. on certain agricultural land at .... (specify).

(B) MEANING OF TERMS

■ 1. 'That you'

Means the identity of the offender.

■ 2. 'being the owner (or person in charge)'

Note that only the owner can commit this offence unless the dog is in the charge of another person, in which case the other would also commit the offence. Where the offence takes place when the dog is in another's charge the owner will not be liable if s/he proves that it was in the charge of some other person whom s/he reasonably believed to be a fit and proper person to be in charge of the dog.

■ 3. 'of a dog which worried'

'Worried' means (a) attacking livestock; or (b) chasing livestock in such a way as may reasonably be expected to cause injury or suffering to the livestock or, in the case of females, abortion, or loss of or diminution in their produce.

■ 4. 'livestock .... (specify)'

'Livestock' means cattle, sheep, goats, swine, horses or poultry; 'cattle' means bulls, cows, oxen, heifers or calves; 'horses' includes asses and mules; 'poultry' means domestic fowls, turkeys, geese or ducks.

■ 5. 'on certain agricultural land at .... (specify)'.

'Agricultural land' means land used as arable, meadow or grazing land or for the purposes of poultry farming, pig farming, market gardens, allotments, nursery grounds or orchards.

(C) USUAL METHODS OF PROVING THESE POINTS

■ 1. 'That you'

Is proved by identifying the owner or person in charge of the dog. This point sometimes causes problems because of the owner's absence when the dog is worrying hens or sheep etc. In these cases it may be necessary to trace the dog to a particular house and then arrange for any witness(es) to see the dog at the house in order to identify the dog and, thereby, the owner.

■ 2. 'being the owner (or person in charge)'

This point is proved by questions to the defendant such as, 'Are you the owner of this dog?' 'Who buys the dog's food?' or 'Where does the dog sleep or live?' Where it is suspected that the owner had left the dog with another person when the worrying took place, a statement from the owner saying who s/he had left in charge of the dog would be necessary.

■ 3. 'of a dog which worried'

'Worried' is proved by a witness stating s/he saw the dog in question attacking livestock or chasing in such a way as may reasonably be expected adversely to affect the livestock as outlined at (B) 3 ante. A statement may be required from an expert witness to prove the possible effects of chasing. If the owner of the livestock, such as a farmer, is not able to give such evidence, consideration could be given to calling a veterinary surgeon. If the dog is not caught in the act of worrying, circumstantial evidence regarding the dog's condition when finally seen could be important. For example in the case of a hen the dog could be examined for the presence of feathers, blood, hen droppings, mud or hen food etc on its muzzle, paws or body.

■ 4. 'livestock .... (specify)'

Evidence must be available that the animal(s) 'worried' was one mentioned in the definition of 'livestock' as defined at (B) 4 ante

■ 5. 'on certain agricultural land at .... (specify)'.

This point is proved by showing in a witness statement that the land where the 'worrying' took place was land mentioned in the definition of 'agricultural land' at (B)5 of this offence.

(D) SUPPORTING EVIDENCE

A defence is provided under section 1(3) and 1(4) where the livestock trespass on the land in question, unless the owner of the dog sets the dog onto the livestock.

The owner of the dog could escape conviction if s/he shows that the dog was left in the charge of a person who was believed to be a fit and proper person to be in charge.

2. POSSESSING ETC SHOTGUN WITHOUT A CERTIFICATE

Section 2 Firearms Act 1968

(A) POINTS TO PROVE

1. That you 2. not being a person exempted from the requirements of the Firearms Act 1968 3. did have in your possession (or purchase or acquire) a shotgun 4. without holding a certificate under the said Act authorising you to possess shotguns.

(B) MEANING OF TERMS

■ 1. 'That you'

Means the identity of the person possessing the shotgun.

■ 2. 'not being a person exempted from the requirements of the Firearms Act 1968'

Briefly, exempted persons include those:

(a) in possession of a police permit;
(b) firearms dealers or their employees;
(c) auctioneers, carriers or warehousemen etc;
(d) licensed slaughtermen etc;
(e) possessing for sporting, athletic and other approved activities, eg at rifle club or range;
(f) borrowing shotguns from an occupier to use on the private premises of the occupier in his/her presence;

(g) shooting at artificial targets with a shotgun with police approval;
(h) using firearms in connection with the theatre and/or cinema;
(i) using firearms connected with equipment for ships and aircraft;
(j) with a visitor's firearm permit issued under section 17 of the 1988 Act;
(k) holding Northern Irish certificates for shotguns.

Note that an antique firearm will not be a shotgun for the purposes of this offence. Whether the shotgun is antique will be a question of fact and degree in each case. However, if it is honestly and reasonably believed to be an antique it matters not if it is not in fact an antique.

■ 3. 'did have in your possession (or purchase, or acquire) a shotgun'

'Possession' used in this offence means having control and would probably cover the much wider circumstances of possession than the phrase 'has with him' would allow. Possession at home or elsewhere would most likely suffice.

'Shotgun' is defined as a smooth-bore gun within the meaning of this Act, that is to say, a smooth-bore gun which has a barrel not less than 24 inches in length and does not have a barrel with a bore exceeding two inches in diameter and either has no magazine or has a non-detachable magazine incapable of holding more than two cartridges and is not a revolver gun. This definition under the Firearms (Amendment) Act 1988 effectively makes into section one firearms, cannons, pump-action and semi-automatic shotguns with a magazine capacity of more than two cartridges and bolt-action shotguns having any capacity of more than two cartridges.

■ 4. 'without holding a certificate under the said Act authorising you to possess shotguns'.

'Shotgun certificate' under this Act means a certificate granted by a chief officer of police under this Act and authorising a person to possess shotguns.

(C) USUAL METHODS OF PROVING THESE POINTS

■ 1. 'That you'

Is proved by identifying the defendant in a witness statement. These offences generally come to light when outstanding renewals of shotgun certificates are enquired into, therefore the witness concerned will usually be the officer dealing with the case.

■ 2. 'not being a person exempted from the requirements of the Firearms Act 1968'

This point would be put forward by the defendant and it would be for the prosecution to disprove the alleged exemption. For example, if a false allegation was made to the effect that s/he had borrowed the shotgun under the exemption as at point (B)2(f) of this offence, the prosecution would try to disprove the claim by taking a statement from the occupier of the land.

■ 3. 'did have in your possession (or purchase or acquire) a shotgun'

Usually proved by a witness stating the defendant was carrying the shotgun or it was found at his/her home or in his/her car. Proving that the firearm in question is a shotgun should not cause problems, but if in doubt expert evidence could be sought.

■ 4. 'without holding a certificate under the said Act authorising you to possess shotguns'.

This point is similar in type to the proving of a 'no insurance' offence under the Road Traffic Act, that is, a defendant could have obtained a shotgun certificate from any one of several chief officers of police, or insurance from one of many companies. In order to save the prosecution the almost impossible task of proving the defendant was not the holder of a certificate, a negative averment can be made. This means that the onus is on the defendant to prove s/he has such a certificate as that particular knowledge is peculiar to him. The prosecution evidence will, therefore, usually consist of a witness stating that the defendant was unable to produce a certificate and/or admitted s/he did not have such a certificate.

3. DISCHARGING FIREARM NEAR HIGHWAY

Section 161(2) Highways Act 1980

(A) POINTS TO PROVE

1. That you 2. did, without lawful authority or excuse 3. discharge a firearm 4. within 50 feet of the centre of .... 5. a highway which comprises (or consists of) a carriageway 6. in consequence whereof users of the highway (or (specify person) a user of the highway) were (or was) injured (or interrupted, or endangered).

(B) MEANING OF TERMS

■ **1. 'That you'** Means the identity of the offender.

■ **2. 'did, without lawful authority or excuse'**

Means that the defendant had no authority under the law, eg a policeman in the execution of his/her duty when killing an escaped bullock on a highway. 'Excuse' could for example apply to the owner of livestock killing a stray dog within 50 feet of the centre of a highway to stop the dog worrying his/her sheep.

■ **3. 'discharge a firearm'**

In the absence of a case to the contrary, discharge apparently means to fire the gun or firearm, and firearm apparently means any lethal barrelled weapon of any description from which any shot, bullet or other missile can be discharged.

■ **4. 'within 50 feet of the centre of .... '**

This distance is measured from the centre of the carriageway in question and the discharging must take place within that distance. (Fifty feet equals 15.24 metres.)

■ **5. 'a highway which comprises (or consists of) a carriageway'**

'Carriageway' means a way contributing to or comprised in a highway, being a way (other than a cycle track) over which the public have a right of way for the passage of vehicles (Highways Act 1980). Therefore footpaths etc on which the public cannot take vehicles are not 'carriageways'.

■ 6. 'in consequence whereof users of the highway (or (specify person) a user of the highway) were (or was) injured (or interrupted, or endangered)'.

This point means that as a result of the discharge of the firearm any user(s) of the highway were:

(a) actually injured; or
(b) interrupted - for example, having to take a different route or take shelter etc; or
(c) endangered - for example, any missile passing near to the user(s) so as to be dangerous.

(C) USUAL METHODS OF PROVING THESE POINTS

■ 1. 'That you'

Is proved by a witness identifying the defendant.

■ 2. 'did, without lawful authority or excuse'

This point is for the defence to raise and, if raised, for the prosecution to disprove.

■ 3. 'discharge a firearm'

Can be proved by a witness stating in his/her statement of evidence that s/he saw and heard etc the defendant fire the gun. The defendant might admit discharging the gun or circumstantial evidence (such as broken street lamps and panes of glass in bus shelter windows or dented cars etc) might be of assistance.

■ 4. 'within 50 feet of the centre of .... '

This point is proved by measuring the 50 feet from the centre of the carriageway and showing, perhaps in the police officer's statement, how far the distance extended. The physical position of the defendant should then be proved to be within the required 50 feet. This could be done in the statement of perhaps another witness who actually saw where the defendant was standing or, failing this, the position could be proved from the defendant's own admission.

■ 5. 'a highway which comprises (consists of) a carriageway'

This point is proved by showing the public had a right of way for the passage of vehicles (being other than a cycle track) in accordance with the definition at point (B)5 of this offence. For example '.......... within 50 feet of the centre of Regent's Street'.

■ **6. 'in consequence whereof users of the highway (or (specify person) a user of the highway) were (or was) injured (or interrupted, or endangered)'.**

Is proved by showing in a witness statement for example: 'I was hit by an air-gun pellet on my left forearm, which caused a slight cut, while walking in High Street' or, 'I had to duck to avoid being hit by air-gun pellets when I cycled in Queen's Street. I was in danger of being hit by a pellet'.

(D) SUPPORTING EVIDENCE

Note. The offences of trespassing with a firearm contrary to section 20 Firearms Act 1968 and carrying a firearm in a public place contrary to section 19 Firearms Act 1968 are both similar to the Highways Act offence. But the Highways Act offence fills the gap where the defendant is neither trespassing (section 20) nor in a public place (section 19), for example when in his/her own front garden.

4. DRINKING UNDER AGE

'Section 150(1) Licensing Act 2003

(A) POINTS TO PROVE

1. That you 2. being a person under 18, namely.......... years old, 3. did on relevant premises 4. knowingly 5. consume 6. alcohol.'

(B) MEANING OF TERMS

■ **1. 'That you'**

Means the person consuming the alcohol.

■ **2. 'being a person under 18 namely .... years'**

Means that the eighteenth birthday has not yet been attained.

A person attains a particular age at the commencement of the relevant anniversary of the date of his/her birth, per section 9 Family Law Reform Act 1969.

■ '3. 'did on relevant premises'

This point is defined by section 159 of the Licensing Act 2003 viz 'relevant premises' means, (a) licensed premises, or (b) premises in respect of which there is in force a club premises certificate, or (c) premises which may be used for a permitted temporary activity by virtue of Part 5 of the Act.

This definition makes it clear that 'drinking under age' can be committed in a public house, club or in premises being used for 'permitted temporary activities' ie the old 'occasional licence' used for wedding receptions, parties indoor or outdoors in a park or a street, etc.

■ 4. 'knowingly'

This point was not in the similar offence under the 1964 Act. This point usually means 'intentionally' as opposed to 'accidentally' or 'unknowingly' ie a *mens rea,* but the courts may provide more explanations in the years to come. Deliberately closing ones eyes could amount to 'knowledge'.

■ 5. 'consume'

This normally means to drink, but as the dictionary definition is 'to use up' or to 'use a commodity' a wider meaning than 'drink', may apply. It would probably include taking into the body via the mouth or nose, eg with a straw or mixed with food etc.

■ 6. 'alcohol'

Means spirits, wine, beer, cider or any other fermented, distilled or spirituous liquor, but excludes, among other things:

(a) alcohol not exceeding 0.5% at the time of the sale or supply in question and

(b) alcohol contained in liqueur confectionery.

See section 191 Licensing Act 2003 for the full definition of alcohol. Shandy (half beer and half lemonade) could well be 'alcohol' as it would normally be over 0.5% in volume of alcohol.

(C) USUAL METHODS OF PROVING THESE POINTS

■ 1. 'That you'

Identification by the police officer.

■ 2. 'being a person under 18 namely............ years'

The vast majority of under-age drinking offences are detected during routine visits to public houses by a sergeant and one or two constables. Persons who are consuming in the bar and who look under 18 may be asked 'What is your date of birth?' Their answer can be recorded in the officer's pocket book together with the result of a check of the suspected offender's birth certificate. In cases of difficulty a statement from someone present at the birth is good evidence.

■ '3. 'did on relevant premises'

This point is proved by referring to the premises concerned as 'licensed premises', 'club' or 'premises used for a permitted temporary activity', as the case may be, eg: 'At 14.40 hours on Friday 26 September xxxx I entered the lounge of the Bulls Head, Main Street, Sometown.' If there is any doubt that the premises fall within the definition of 'relevant premises' the appropriate licence should be examined. Failure to produce the licence or a certified copy (without reasonable excuse) is an offence (section 57(5)).

Under Section 180 there is a right of entry using reasonable force if necessary for a constable. There must be reason to believe an offence under the Act has been, is being or is about to be committed.

■ 4. ' knowingly'.

This point would normally be proved by asking the suspect what s/he or she was drinking. Any admission that showed knowledge of alcohol would suffice, eg 'a lager, beer or wine' etc. This is an additional hurdle for the police to prove compared to the old offence and where there is doubt, statements may be required from bar staff or other witnesses to show the extent of the suspect's knowledge. The state of the suspect's mind is for the court to decide. NB Be aware of a later defence that someone 'spiked' the drink or there had been a mistake.

■ 5. 'consume'

As for (C)4 above, asking what s/he was drinking or seeing the person drink would prove this point.

■ 6. 'alcohol'

This can be proved by asking the suspect as at (C)4 above, by smelling the drink, by statements from the bar staff or in extreme cases by seizing the drink for analysis.

(D) SUPPORTING EVIDENCE

There is a defence to this offence of 'drinking under age' provided by section 150(4) which states section 150(1) does not apply where:

- the person is 16 or 17 years of age;
- the alcohol is beer, wine or cider;
- drunk at a table meal on 'relevant premises', and
- the person accompanied at the meal by one aged 18 or over.

5. FOUND DRUNK

Section 12 Licensing Act 1872

(A) POINTS TO PROVE

1. That you 2. were found 3. drunk 4. in a highway (or other public place or certain premises licensed for the sale of intoxicating liquors by retail) called............

(B) MEANING OF TERMS

■ 1. 'That you' Means the identity of the accused.

■ 2. 'were found'

Means that for the offence to be committed the officer etc must 'find' the accused in a drunken state. The offence was designed to provide protection for the drunken person etc, so that, when sober, the accused could not be reported for his/her drunkenness.

In *Winzar v Chief Constable of Kent* (1983) *Times* March 28, it was held that lawfully ejecting a drunk from a hospital into a public place did not negate being found drunk on a highway.

■ 3. 'drunk'

This point means under the influence of alcohol to such an extent that a police officer would feel that the defendant was a liability to him/herself or other persons or property. Section 24 PACE 1984 could be considered, ie to arrest a person where there are reasonable grounds for believing it is necessary to prevent injury (see 'Arrest' at end of book under 'Powers'). Consider taking such offenders to a detoxification centre or a penalty notice for disorder.

■ 4. 'in a highway (or other public place or certain premises licensed for the sale of intoxicating liquors by retail) called......'.

'Highway' and 'licensed premises' are widely understood and, normally, cause no problems. Note that an occasional licence is included in the term 'licensed premises'.

'Other public place' means places other than highways to which the public have access whether on payment or otherwise. Persons found drunk inside a tramcar or hackney carriage would probably come within this offence.

(C) USUAL METHODS OF PROVING THESE POINTS

■ 1. 'That you'

Is proved by the officer dealing with the case identifying the defendant in his/her statement of evidence.

■ 2. 'were found' This point is proved by the officer dealing with the case including in his/her statement words such as, 'I found the defendant on the pavement in the High Street'.

■ 3. 'drunk'

This point could be proved in the officer's statement by words, such as, 'Unsteady on his feet; could not walk; glassy eyed; breath smelling of alcohol; speech slurred; vomited on his clothing; urinated in his trousers' etc. All help to describe drunkenness or being drunk and incapable.

■ 4. 'in a highway (or other public place or certain premises licensed for the sale of intoxicating liquors by retail) called.............'.

This point is proved by describing in the officer's statement the place where the defendant was found, ie (a) a 'highway' such as King Street, or Oxford Street; or (b) 'other public place' such as a football ground or railway station; or (c) 'licensed premises' such as the Three Legs public house or the Swan and Talbot Inn.

6. DRUNK AND DISORDERLY

Section 91(1) Criminal Justice Act 1967

(A) POINTS TO PROVE

1. That you 2. while drunk 3. in any public place namely .... 4. were guilty of disorderly behaviour.

(B) MEANING OF TERMS

■ 1. 'That you'

Means the identity of the defendant.

■ 2. 'while drunk'

Means that the defendant was under the influence of alcohol to such an extent that a police officer would feel that s/he could be described as drunk. Sniffing glue or taking drugs would not amount to being 'drunk'.

■ 3. 'in any public place, namely ....'

'Public place' is defined as including any highway and any other premises or place to which at the material time the public have or are permitted to have access, whether on payment or otherwise (section 91(4) Criminal Justice Act 1967). Such places as the public rooms of licensed premises during permitted hours and railway stations will be public places.

■ 4. 'were guilty of disorderly behaviour'.

There is no definition of this term but it is submitted that any conduct which is not orderly, such as a breach of the peace, would suffice. For example, shouting, waving arms about and interfering with other people's comfort would probably amount to disorderly behaviour.

(C) USUAL METHODS OF PROVING THESE POINTS

■ 1. 'That you'

Is usually proved by the police officer who is dealing with the case identifying the defendant.

■ 2. 'while drunk'

This point is usually proved in the police officer's statement by sentences such as, 'unsteady on his feet, glassy eyes, breath smelling of alcohol, speech slurred, untidy clothing, vomit on clothing, urinated in trousers etc'.

■ 3. 'in any public place namely............'

This point could be established by describing in the police officer's statement the place where the defendant was disorderly, eg, 'In High Street, at the first division football ground of............', 'in the bar of the Red Lion during permitted hours etc'. In cases involving public places where the public are only admitted on payment etc the prosecution must prove that the place comes within the definition of public place at (B)3 of this offence. The landing of a block of flats was held not to be a 'public place' where admittance was gained by key, security code etc (*Williams (Richard) v DPP* [1992] Crim LR 503.

■ 4. 'were guilty of disorderly behaviour'.

Established by observations in the police officer's statement to the effect. 'I told him to be quiet and go home but he refused, started shouting "Nazis, Nazis", and waved his arms about', or, 'I saw him trying to jump over the railings near the market place traffic lights and a crowd of people began to gather. I told him to stop and go home but he continued trying to jump the railings etc', or, 'I saw him pushing his way into a taxi queue and shouting "I am having the first taxi", I told him to go home quietly but he refused to stop pushing in front of people... etc'.

(D) SUPPORTING EVIDENCE

The arresting officer may take the offender to a treatment centre for alcoholics per section 34 Criminal Justice Act 1972.

7. LITTER OFFENCE

Section 87 Environmental Protection Act 1990
as amended by section 18 Clean Neighbourhoods
and Environment Act 2005

(A) POINTS TO PROVE

1. That you 2. did throw down (or drop or otherwise deposit) 3. 'any litter' 4. 'in any place which is open to the air' 5. 'and left it'.

(B) MEANING OF TERMS

■ 1. 'That you'

Means the identity of the offender.

■ 2. 'did throw down (or drop or otherwise deposit)'

Means any method of 'depositing' litter.

In *Felix v DPP* [1998] Crim LR 657 it was held that 'otherwise deposits' had a wide meaning and 'deposits' means no more than 'places' or 'puts'.

■ 3. 'any litter'

Apart from the dictionary definition the legislators have left the meaning open but add that: 'Litter includes (a) the discarded ends of cigarettes, cigars and like products, and (b) discarded chewing-gum and the discarded remains of other products designed for chewing.' Human/animal faeces and anything in a relatively stable form would also be 'litter.'

■ 4. 'in any place which is open to the air'

This extends the old litter offence to all open places, but not if the public doesn't have paid or unpaid access. The place may be on land or water, or covered (provided it is open on at least one side S86(13). Beaches to the low-water mark are included.' This section applies to any place 'in the area of a Principal Litter Authority (PLA)' open to the air with public access. PLAs are County Councils, County Borough or District Councils, a London Borough Council, the Common Council of the City of London and the Isles of Scilly Council. See also 'relevant land' etc under sections 86(4)- (15) and 87.

■ 5. 'and left it'

This point means 'left' and not necessarily 'abandoned' (*Witney v Cattanach* [1979] Crim LR 461). In this case the defendant was living in a tent near his lorry with his wife and seven children. He sorted through a pile of metal beside his parked lorry. It was held that the metal had been deposited and permitted to remain beside the road for such a time and in such circumstances that it could be said to have been left there. An article deposited with no intention to remove it could be found to have been left after it had been there only a short time.

(C) USUAL METHODS OF PROVING THESE POINTS

■ 1. 'That you'

Is usually proved by a witness identifying the defendant etc.

■ 2. 'did throw down (or drop or otherwise deposit)'

This point is usually proved by a witness stating that, 'I saw [the defendant] throw the fish and chip papers out of her car window on to the road', or, 'I saw [the defendant] throw a newspaper into my garden from the adjoining road'.

■ 3. 'any litter'

The type of litter is proved in the witness statement or by the admission of the offender. Eg 'I saw the plastic food container thrown out of the car window and land on the pavement of Queen Street. The car drove off but its number was....'

■ 4. 'In any place which is open to the air'

This can be proved in the witness statement by showing it was not in a building or under a tent etc. It is argued that a three-sided bus shelter would be open to the air, but it is for the courts to decide on these less obvious circumstances.

■ 5. 'and left it'

The prosecution must be careful to show that the defendant had not just thrown down litter which s/he intended to collect later and dispose of lawfully. In the majority of cases the 'leaving' will be obvious, but help could be obtained from the decision in *Witney v Cattanach* at (B)5 of this offence in cases of difficulty.

(D) SUPPORTING EVIDENCE

A defence to the litter offence can be found at section 87 (4A and 4B), to wit:

'Sub-section (4)A' - No offence is committed under sub-section (1) above where the depositing of the litter is:

- (a) authorised by law: or
- (b) done by or with the consent of the owner, occupier or other person having control of the place where it is deposited.

'Sub-section (4)B' - A person may only give consent under paragraph (4A)(b) above in relation to the depositing of litter in a lake or pond or watercourse if s/he is the owner, occupier or other person having control of:

- (a) all the land adjoining that lake or pond or watercourse; and
- (b) all the land through or into which water in that lake or pond or watercourse directly or indirectly discharges, otherwise than by means of a public sewer.

See the Water Resources Act 1991 for definitions of 'Lake or pond,' 'watercourse' and 'public sewer'.

8. SPORTING EVENTS - CONTROL OF ALCOHOL

Section 2(1) Sporting Events (Control of Alcohol etc) Act 1985

(A) POINTS TO PROVE

1. That you 2. had intoxicating liquor (or an article to which this section applies) 3. in your possession 4. at a time during the period of a designated sporting event 5. while being in an area of a designated sports ground from which the event may be directly viewed, namely,.............

(B) MEANING OF TERMS

■ 1. 'That you'

Means the person who is in possession of intoxicating liquor.

■ 2. 'had intoxicating liquor (or an article to which this section applies)'

'Intoxicating liquor' has the same meaning as under section 201(1) Licensing Act 1964 (see offence 4(B)6, Drinking under age). 'Intoxicating liquor' is to be changed to 'alcohol' by the Licensing Act 2003 on a date to be fixed.

This section applies to any article capable of causing injury to a person struck by it, being :

(a) a bottle, can or other portable container (including such an article when crushed or broken) which -
  (i) is for holding any drink, and
  (ii) is of a kind, which, when empty, is normally discarded or returned to, or left to be recovered by, the supplier; or
(b) part of an article falling within paragraph (a) above: but does not apply to anything that is for holding any medical product (within the meaning of the Medicines Act).

■ 3. 'in your possession' 'Possession' appears to mean actually in the physical possession of the offender.

■ 4. 'at a time during the period of a designated sporting event'

A **'designated sporting event'** means an event or proposed event which has been designated or is part of a class designated by order made by the Secretary of State. It also includes events designated under comparable Scottish legislation. Events which are to be held outside Great Britain can also be designated.

The 'period of a designated sporting event' means the period of time commencing two hours before the start of the event and ending one hour after the end of it. However if the start is delayed then the period commencing two hours before the advertised start is included. If an event is postponed or cancelled then the period in such a case is the period commencing two hours before the advertised start and ending one hour after that time.

'Designation of sports grounds and events' are dealt with as follows... The Sports Grounds and Sporting Events (Designation) Order 2005 designated the sports grounds and sporting events to which the Act applies.

The 'designated grounds' are any designated sports ground in England or Wales (see B5 following).

Definition of **'designated matches'**. For the purposes of the Sporting Events (Control of Alcohol etc) Act 1985, the Sports Grounds and Sporting Events (Designation) Order 2005 revoked and replaced the 1985 Order of the same name.

The 2005 Order designates sporting events to which the Act applies:

1. Association football matches in which one or both of the participating teams represents a club which is for the time being a member (whether a full or associate member) of the Football League, the Football Association Premier League, the Football Conference National Division, the Scottish Football League or Welsh Premier League, or represents a country or territory at any sports ground in England or Wales.

2. Association football matches in competition for the Football Association Cup (other than in a preliminary or qualifying round) at any sports ground in England or Wales.
3. Association football matches at a sports ground outside England and Wales in which one or both of the participating teams represents a club which is for the time being a member (whether a full or associate member) of the Football League, the Football Association Premier League, the Football Conference National division, the Scottish Football League or Welsh Premier League, or represents the Football Association or the Football Association of Wales.

The Act does not apply to any sporting event or proposed sporting event where all competitors are to take part otherwise than for reward, and to which all spectators are to be admitted free of charge.

■ 5. 'while being in an area of a designated sports ground from which the event may be directly viewed, namely, ...'.

A 'designated sports ground' means any place used for sporting events which has accommodation for spectators and which has been designated or is part of a class designated by the Secretary of State. The area of a ground from which an event may be directly viewed includes stands, terraces and any restaurants, sponsors' boxes and other rooms which overlook the pitch.
'Namely' would require a description of the place where the offender was seen, eg 'at the front of the stand in seat A24'.

(C) USUAL METHODS OF PROVING THESE POINTS

■ 1. 'That you'

This point is normally proved by the police officer in his/her statement of evidence. For example: 'I saw a man I know to be Bob Robinson sitting in seat A24…'

■ 2. 'had intoxicating liquor (or an article to which this section applies)'

The proof that a substance is intoxicating liquor will be similar to that required in offence 5 (Drinking under age). The question should be asked: 'What are you drinking?' In cases of difficulty the drink should be analysed by experts.

■ 3. 'in your possession'

The police officer's evidence would prove this point, eg, 'I saw Mr Robinson holding a can of beer'.

■ 4. 'at a time during the period of a designated sporting event'.

This can be proved by showing in the police officer's statement that the game being played was an association football match between two Football League clubs namely............

'During the period' can be proved by showing that the offence took place between the specified times, eg, 'The football game had begun 15 minutes before the offence'.

■ 5. 'while being in an area of a designated sports ground from which the event may be directly viewed, namely ....'.

'Designated sports ground' can be proved by including in the police officer's statement of evidence that the match was being played on the home ground of the Sometime United Football Club, a Football Association club.

'Directly viewed' can be proved by the police officer showing in his/her statement words to the effect that the pitch could be directly viewed from the stand where Mr Robinson was sitting.

(D) SUPPORTING EVIDENCE

Note 1. Medical products as mentioned under (B)2 of this offence include substances which can be administered to animals for medical purposes.

9. TRESPASSING ON LAND

Section 61 Criminal Justice and Public Order Act 1994

(A) POINTS TO PROVE

1. That you 2. knowing 3. that a direction under subsection (1) of this section had been given 4. which applied to you 5. failed to leave the land 6. as soon as was reasonably practicable or 7. having left, again entered the land as a trespasser 8. within a period of three months 9. beginning with the day on which the direction was given.

(B) MEANING OR TERMS

■ **1. 'That you'** Means the identity of the offender.

■ **2. 'knowing'**

Means that guilty knowledge is required and that the offender must be aware of the next point.

■ **3. 'that a direction under subsection (1) had been given'**

The 'direction' means that where a senior police officer present at the scene reasonably believes that:

(a) two or more persons are trespassing on land AND are present there with the common purpose of residing there for any period;

(a) that reasonable steps have been taken by or on behalf of the occupier, to ask them to leave;

AND

(a) that any of those persons has caused damage to the land or property thereon OR used threatening, abusive or insulting words or behaviour towards the occupier, a member of his/her family or an employee or agent of his, or

(b) that those persons have between them six or more vehicles on the land;

he (the senior police officer) may DIRECT those persons, or any of them, to leave the land and to remove any vehicles or other property they have with them on the land.

■ 4. 'which applied to you'

Means that the above direction applied to the offender.

■ 5. 'failed to leave the land ....'

Means in effect, not vacating the land described together with any vehicle or property s/he might have there.

■ 6. 'as soon as reasonably practicable'

Means that if the trespasser has accumulated a lot of property on the land then common sense must prevail in allowing sufficient time for vacation.

■ 7. 'having left, entered the land again as a trespasser'

Means that the leaving was not final and that the trespasser had entered the same piece of land again, section 61(4).

■ 8.'within a period of three months'

Means three calendar months.

■ 9. 'beginning with the day on which the direction was given'.

The three calendar months starts with the day the trespasser was told to leave. Presumably no offence under section 61(4) will be committed if the trespasser returns after three months.

(C) USUAL METHODS OF PROVING THESE POINTS

■ 1. 'That you'

Can be proved by asking the person his/her name and date of birth etc during the interview. Photographs or video could be considered or even the power of arrest where identity is a problem.

■ 2. 'knowing'

Can be proved by asking the trespasser if s/he was aware that s/he had been directed to leave the land. If the trespasser is not co-operative then a statement from the officer giving or communicating news of the direction, or some other witness, could help prove this point.

■ 3. 'that a direction under subsection (1) etc has been given.'

This point would be best proved by an admission from the trespasser that the direction had been given or from a statement from the officer giving the direction.

■ 4. 'which applied to you'
Can be proved in a statement from the occupier of the land or the officer dealing with the case, to the effect that the direction was made, was communicated and was pertinent to the trespasser or during the interview with the trespasser.

■ 5. 'failed to leave the land
Would be obvious to all concerned and a statement to that effect from a witness would suffice fully describing the land eg – 'The five-acre field adjacent to Plum Tree Farm'.

■ 6. 'as soon as reasonably practicable'
This point can be proved by setting a reasonable period for the trespasser to vacate the land and showing such a period in the police officer's statement - OR

■ 7. 'having left again enters the land as a trespasser'
Can be proved by showing in the police officer's statement or some other witness' statement that the trespasser left the land but entered again without permission, ie as a trespasser.

■ 8. 'within a period of three months'
Proved by showing the date on which the direction to leave was given and the date of re-entry in a witness' statement.

■ 9. 'beginning with the day on which the direction was given'.
Proved as above.

(D) SUPPORTING EVIDENCE

Note 1. Section 61(2) of the Criminal Justice and Public Order Act 1994 also provides that where the senior police officer believes that the persons on the land were not originally trespassers - but have since become trespassers - the officer must reasonably believe that the subsection (1) conditions are satisfied after those persons become trespassers, before s/he can give a subsection (1) direction.

The subsection (1) conditions include damage or threats etc (see (B)3 of this offence) and note that damage includes the deposit of any substance capable of polluting the land.

Once the direction has been given, any police officer at the scene (not just the senior police officer) can communicate news of it to the trespassers.

Note 2. A defence is provided viz: if the accused shows s/he was not trespassing on the land or that s/he had a reasonable excuse for failing to leave the land as soon as reasonably practicable or for re-entering the land as a trespasser. Such reasonable excuses could be the presence of the elderly, invalids, pregnant women, children etc and the police may wish to take such matters into account when dealing with this offence.

Note 3. Among other definitions, 'vehicle' is defined as any vehicle, whether or not fit for road use, and includes any chassis or body with or without wheels, appearing to have formed part of such a vehicle and any load carried by, and anything attached to, such a vehicle; AND any caravan, which means any structure designed or adapted for human habitation, capable of being moved from one place to another by towing or being transported on a motor vehicle or trailer and any motor vehicle so designed or adapted (but not a tent or railway rolling stock).

10. TICKET TOUT OFFENCE

Section 166 Criminal Justice and Public Order Act 1994

(A) POINTS TO PROVE

1. That you, 2. being an unauthorised person 3. did sell, or offer or expose for sale, 4. a ticket for a designated football match, namely .... 5. in any public place or place to which the public has access or 6. in the course of a trade or business, in any other place.

(B) MEANING OF TERMS

■ 1. 'That you'

Means the identity of the ticket tout.

■ 2. 'being an unauthorised person'
This is defined as 'a person is "unauthorised" unless s/he is authorised in writing to sell tickets for the match by the home club or by the organisers of the match'.

■ 3. 'did sell, or offer or expose for sale'
The normal places for touts are outside the ground in question before the game or alongside the queues waiting for tickets. Sale etc will be obvious from the actions of the tout and his/her customers. Money should normally change hands for a sale or the tout's sales patter will show an offering or exposing for sale.

In theory an exposing for sale could be committed by merely showing the tickets to prospective customers, although words or an actual sale would normally be easier to prove.

■ 4. 'a ticket for a designated football match, namely ....'
'Ticket' is defined as anything which purports to be a ticket.
'Designated football match' is defined as a football match, or football match of a description, for the time being designated under Part 1 of the Football Spectators Act 1989. The particular football match should be shown.

■ 5. 'in any public place or place to which the public has access'
Usual places for this offence will be on the street or in public houses or clubs. In the absence of a judicial decision it is considered that a place will still be public even if admission is on payment, eg an outdoor pop concert, agricultural show or point-to-point meeting.

■ 6. 'in the course of a trade or business ....'.
This phrase means that where the tout sells etc in the course of a trade or business then the offence can be committed anywhere, such as in the privacy of a dwelling house.

(C) USUAL METHODS OF PROVING THESE POINTS

■ 1. 'That you'
This is proved by the officer dealing with the offence, eg, 'I saw a man, I now know to be Ashley Jackson, in Elland

Road, Leeds outside Leeds United Football Club...' The reasons for knowing Ashley Jackson would be from his car, by examining his driving licence, passport or visiting his house or talking to his neighbours or a combination of those or other similar things. In difficult cases it should be borne in mind that an arrest may be necessary.

■ 2. 'being an unauthorised person'

This point can be proved by asking the suspect, 'Have you any authority or permission to sell those tickets?'

This could be backed up by taking statements from the home club or the match organisers to show they hadn't given written permission as required by the Act.

■ 3.'did sell, or offer or expose for sale'

These verbs can be proved by observations of a plain clothes officer who could say in his/her statement that s/he saw money change hands, the tout walking up and down the queue of football supporters shouting out his/her prices or merely showing a selection of tickets in his/her hand to the persons in the queue.

Further evidence could be obtained by taking statements from persons in the queue.

■ 4. 'a ticket for a designated football match, namely ....'

The 'ticket' can be seized for evidence whether it is an actual ticket or a forgery and shown as an exhibit in the officer's statement of evidence. Note that the police power of search and entry will include a vehicle reasonably believed to be used in the offence. A football match can be proved to be designated by referring to the Football (Offences) Act 1991.

■ 5. 'in any public place or place to which the public had access'

The proof of this point can be made by the officer in the case describing the place, eg, 'In High Street outside the Craig Thompson Ticket Agents Office'. In cases where doubt exists, such as the foyer of the ticket office, statements from the owner or occupier of the premises would be beneficial.

■ 6. 'in the course of a trade or business in any other place'.
It would be necessary to show the tout was running a trade or business. If this is denied by the tout, such things as advertising in local papers, shop windows, letter heads or business cards, telephone company records and tax returns or VAT registration might help prove this point. Once it is proved that the tout is trading then any other place is included.

(D) SUPPORTING EVIDENCE

Note. The Home Secretary has power in this section for the discretionary making of an order to extend this offence to sporting events for which 6,000 or more tickets are issued for sale.

11. TAXI TOUT OFFENCE

Section 167 Criminal Justice and Public Order Act 1994

(A) POINTS TO PROVE

1. That you 2. did solicit persons 3. in a public place, namely .... 4. to hire vehicles 5. to carry them as passengers.

(B) MEANING OF TERMS

■ 1. 'That you'

Means the identity of the person soliciting.

■ 2. 'did solicit persons'

Means to incite or induce persons. The mere display of a sign on a vehicle that the vehicle is for hire does not amount to soliciting. Plying for hire, contrary to the Town Police Clauses Act could be considered.

■ 3. 'in a public place'

Means any highway and 'any other premises or place to which at the material time the public have or are permitted to have access (whether on payment or otherwise)'.

■ 4. 'to hire vehicles'

Means a borrowing for a price. Borrowing is normally free but a borrowing for money or other consideration is a contract of hire. 'Vehicle' is defined in the glossary ante.

■ 5. 'to carry them as passengers'.

This phrase means to transport a person or persons from A to B. However, as the offence we are dealing with is complete with the mere soliciting, there is no need for an actual hiring or carrying of passenger.

(C) USUAL METHODS OF PROVING THESE POINTS

■ 1. 'That you'

Usually proved by the officer who witnessed the soliciting/touting.

■ 2. 'did solicit persons'

This point can be proved by admission during interview and/or from what the witnesses saw. The offender might give out business cards, display leaflets, talk to people waiting for legitimate taxis or drive around in a vehicle inciting or encouraging people to hire him/her for a lift home etc. Any printed or written word used by the offender should be seized for evidence and appear as an exhibit in the police officer's statement.

■ 3. 'in a public place, namely ....'

This point is normally proved by naming the street in the officer's statement. When difficulty is foreseen, such as private premises where for that day the public have access on payment of £5 each, then a statement from an organiser of the event may be necessary.

■ 4. 'to hire vehicles'

Can be proved from what the offender said or displayed during the 'soliciting' eg, 'We'll take you for half the taxi fare' or, 'We aren't more expensive after midnight'.

Note that some money or consideration must be mentioned or implied in the inciting.

■ 5. 'to carry them as passengers'.
This phrase, like the previous one, is proved from what the offender says or displays during the soliciting. Admissions during the police interview or from what witnesses to the incitement heard the defendant say or saw him/her do are the usual ways of proving this point.

(D) SUPPORTING EVIDENCE

If the soliciting is in pursuance of a special shared taxi scheme under the Transport Act 1985, then the above offence does not apply. It is a defence to show that the soliciting was for passengers for public services vehicles on behalf of the holder of a PSV operator's licence and with that person's authority.

12. POACHING AT NIGHT

Section 1 Night Poaching Act 1828

(A) POINTS TO PROVE

1. That you 2. did by night 3. unlawfully enter (or be on land), whether open or enclosed 4. with a gun (net, engine, or other instrument) 5. for the purpose of taking or destroying 6. game.

(B) MEANING OF TERMS

■ 1. 'That you' Means the identity of the poacher.
■ 2. 'did by night' 'Night' is defined as commencing at the expiration of the first hour after sunset and concluding at the beginning of the last hour before sunrise.
■ 3. 'unlawfully enter (or be on) land whether open or enclosed'
This point means a personal entry as opposed to a constructive entry by the poacher's dog. Open land appears to be land without hedges, walls or fences and enclosed land would appear to have some means of enclosure.

■ 4. 'with a gun (net, engine, or other instrument)'

Note that a dog is not included within this offence, therefore a person who enters land for the purpose of taking game solely with a dog does not commit this offence (unless s/he also has a gun, net, engine or other instrument). If s/he is successful with the dog alone and takes game s/he would commit the offence of taking game by night, also contrary to section 1 Night Poaching Act 1828.

■ 5. 'for the purpose of taking or destroying'

This means that the purpose for him/her being on the land is the taking alive or killing of the game.

■ 6. 'game'.

'Game' is defined as hares, pheasants, partridges, grouse, heath or moor game, black game and bustards. Note that rabbits are not game' under this Act, ie they are included in the offence of actually taking game (or rabbits) but are not included in the merely 'entering on land' offence.

(C) USUAL METHODS OF PROVING THESE POINTS

■ 1. 'That you'

This point will probably be proved by the witness who found the poacher, eg the gamekeeper.

■ 2. 'did by night'

This can be proved in the police officer's statement coupled with the witness who actually saw what time the poacher was entering onto the land. Sunrise and sunset should be proved. Where there is any doubt a court can take judicial notice of such times by consulting an almanac.

■ 3. 'unlawfully enter (or be on) land whether open or enclosed.'

This point can be proved by the gamekeeper or other witness to the personal entry on to the land by the poacher. A brief description of the land may help the court, ie whether open or enclosed.

■ 4. 'with a gun (net, engine or other instrument)'

Again the observations of the witnesses will prove this point together with any item seized for evidence.

■ 5. 'for the purpose of taking or destroying'

Only the purpose needs proving not the actual taking of game. This is in the mind of the poacher or his/her accomplices. It will usually be proved by admission from the poacher, but circumstantial evidence may be adequate to show a purpose (or intent) to take or destroy game, for example, possessing all the necessary equipment.

■ 6. 'game'.

Occasionally an expert witness may be needed to identify the particular game, but in the vast majority of cases a statement from a witness or police officer will prove this point.

(D) SUPPORTING EVIDENCE

A constable may enter on land to arrest suspects where there are reasonable grounds for suspecting an offence under this section is being committed (section 24 PACE 1984).

Further powers of search, seizure and forfeiture are under the Game Laws (Amendment) Act 1960, section 4.

13. RAVE OFFENCE

Section 63 Criminal Justice and Public Order Act 1994

(A) POINTS TO PROVE

1. That you 2. knowing that a direction had been given that applied to you 3. failed to leave land as soon as reasonably practicable 4. when a rave was in progress (or in preparation).

(B) MEANING OF TERMS

■ 1. 'That you'

Means the person to whom the direction has been given.

■ 2. 'knowing that a direction had been given that applied to you'

This point is explained at section 63(2) of the CJPO Act as follows. If, as respects any land in the open air, a police officer of at least the rank of superintendent reasonably believes that:

(a) two or more persons are making preparations for the holding there of a gathering to which this section applies,
(b) 10 or more persons are waiting for such a gathering to begin there, or
(c) 10 or more persons are attending such a gathering which is in progress;

he may give a direction that those persons and any other persons who come to prepare or wait for or to attend the gathering are to leave the land and remove any vehicles or other property which they have with them on the land.

If the superintendent does not communicate with all the 'ravers' any constable at the scene may pass on the direction.

To help in proving the mental element of 'knowing', section 63(4) provides that: 'persons shall be treated as having had a direction communicated to them if reasonable steps have been taken to bring it to their attention.'

Therefore any loudhailer broadcast would appear to be a reasonable step.

Note that this direction also applies to vehicles and property eg, amplifiers, speakers, tents, caravans etc.

■ 3. 'failed to leave land as soon as reasonably practicable'

Means that the person(s) who have had the direction communicated to them should move off the land together with any of their property. 'Reasonably practicable' would allow for common sense to prevail where invalids, the old or very young or large amounts of equipment etc are present.

The land must be 'land in the open air' which includes a place partly open to the air, eg a dutch barn (basically a roof supported by four posts).

Persons exempt from leaving the land are the occupier, his/her family or employees or agents and any person whose home is situated on the land.

A defence exists for failing to leave the land as soon as practicable where the accused can show s/he had a reasonable excuse, eg illness or injury or possibly the loss of some valuable object etc.

■ 4. 'when a rave was in progress (or in preparation)'

'Rave' is defined in section 63(1) of the Act:

This section applies to a gathering on land in the open air of 20 or more persons (100 or more in Scotland) (whether or not trespassers), at which amplified music is played during the night (with or without intermissions) and is such as, by reason of its loudness and duration and the time at which it is played, is likely to cause serious distress to the inhabitants of the locality; and for this purpose –

(a) such a gathering continues during intermissions in the music and, where the gathering extends over several days, throughout the period during which amplified music is played at night (with or without intermissions); and
(b) 'music' includes sounds wholly or predominantly characterised by the emission of a succession of repetitive beats.

Once it is considered that such a rave is being planned, the direction can be given to 'nip it in the bud' at the preparation stage or the stage where only ten or more people are present.

(C) USUAL METHODS OF PROVING THESE POINTS

■ 1. 'That you'

This point will be proved by the officer in the case either arresting the offender or identifying him/her for process by summons.

■ 2. 'knowing that a direction had been given that applied to you'

An admission from the accused that s/he knew a direction had been given and that it applied to him/her would be best evidence. Failing that the officer should prove that 'reasonable steps had been taken to bring it to their attention', eg an explanation in his/her statement of what s/he had said to the accused or a statement from the superintendent who had given the original direction.

■ 3. 'failed to leave land as soon as reasonably practicable'

This point could be proved by the officer showing the time of the direction and the fact that some time later the accused was still on the land and taking no steps to leave. The two defences should be borne in mind and questions asked if in doubt, eg, 'Do you or your family live or work on this land?' or 'Have you any reasonable excuse for not leaving this land?'

A description of the land in question should be made in the police officer's statement to prove it was 'land in the open air.'

■ 4. 'when a rave is in progress (or in preparation)'.

The police must prove that the 'gathering' or rave comes within the definition at (B)4 ante. This is easily done when such a gathering is in progress. If it is only in preparation, the superintendent would have to prove that s/he 'reasonably believed' that the gathering would come under section 63.

(D) SUPPORTING EVIDENCE

Note 1. This offence also caters for those who return to the land within a period of seven days beginning with the day on which the direction was given (unless they can show a reasonable excuse for again entering the land).

Note 2. Supplementary powers of entry and seizure are provided in section 64 of the Act. Section 65 provides a power to stop persons from proceeding to raves where a direction under section 63 has been given.

Note 3. All the above only applies to 'land in the open air' and not to premises, buildings, clubs etc.

Section 4

Powers of the Police

POWERS OF THE POLICE

Police powers provide a power of arrest for all offences conditional on **'the necessity'** of the arrest; see PACE Code of Practice G where it explains that when considering individual circumstances, the constable must take into account:

- Victim's situation;
- Investigative processes needs;
- Nature of the offence, and
- Suspect's circumstances (VINS for the memory).

NB: Any power requiring a constable to have reasonable grounds for believing/suspecting makes it imperative that the officer records what the reasonable grounds were!

1. ARREST

The Serious Organised Crime and Police Act 2005 (SOCPA) amends section 24 Pace 1984 viz.

A constable may arrest without warrant:

- anyone about to, or in the act of committing an offence; or
- anyone officer has reasonable grounds for suspecting about to, or in the act of committing an offence; OR
- when an offence has been committed, anyone guilty or officer has reasonable grounds for suspecting guilty of it; or
- if officer has reasonable grounds for suspecting an offence has been committed, anyone s/he has reasonable grounds to suspect of it.

'The necessity principle'

The above powers of arrest can ONLY be used where the officer has reasonable grounds to believe it is **'necessary'** – for any of the following reasons:

1 For the name to be ascertained - constable does not know or reasonable grounds to doubt real name given;
2 For the address to be ascertained - as for 1 above;

3 To prevent suspect –
   - causing physical injury to self or other,
   - suffering physical injury,
   - causing loss or damage to property,
   - committing offence against public decency, ie where public could not be reasonably expected to avoid it,
   - causing unlawful obstruction of highway;

4 To protect child or other vulnerable person from suspect;

5 To allow for prompt and effective investigation of offence or conduct of suspect;

6 To prevent prosecution of offence being hindered by disappearance of suspect.

Under the Serious Organised Crime and Police Act 2005 (SOCPA) section 110(4) these powers of arrest apply to ANY offence WHENEVER committed.

Mnemonic for reasons

D disappearance of suspect
P public decency offence
P protect vulnerable from suspect

P prevent suffering injury
H highways unlawful obstruction
I injury of self or other
I investigation of offence/conduct to allow for effective
A address or name not known
L loss or damage of property **'DPP PHIIAL'**

2. SEIZURE OF MOTOR VEHICLES

To help combat the use of motor vehicles without driving licences or insurance, and to keep pace with the increased use of PNC, DVLA, the Motor Insurance Database and the Automated Number Plate Recognition technology, the following powers have been created.

Under section 152 of the Serious Organised Crime and Police Act 2005 (SOCPA), section 165A is added to the Road Traffic Act 1988 which provides a power to seize motor vehicles driven without a driving licence or insurance if:

- a constable in uniform requires production of driving licence or insurance and – the suspect fails to produce and – the constable has reasonable grounds to believe – that the 'no driving licence or insurance' offence(s) is/are being committed; or
- the constable has required the vehicle to stop and – it failed to stop or stop long enough for enquiries and – constable has reasonable grounds to believe driven with no driving licence or insurance.

If unable to seize because of not stopping or driving off:

- the constable may seize within 24 hours – may enter premises other than dwelling house (note: 'dwelling house' does not include outbuildings or adjacent land) – on which reasonable grounds to believe vehicle is – and may use reasonable force.

Before seizure a WARNING must be given (unless not practicable) that the vehicle will be seized unless the driving licence or insurance is produced immediately.

The law for the removal, retention, release and disposal of the vehicle can be found in the Road Traffic Act 1988 (Retention and Disposal of Seized Motor Vehicles) Regulations, 2005.

Also see the Removal and Disposal of Vehicles (Traffic Officers) (England) Regulations 2008 that empowers 'Highways Agency Traffic Officers' in uniform to remove or require the removal of vehicles that are stationary, broken down or abandoned – from motorways and trunk roads – and roads in the vicinity of or land adjacent to such roads, ie those under control of the Highways Agency.

Also under Regulation 4 Removal and Disposal of Vehicles Regulations 1986, a constable may remove or arrange for the removal of a vehicle – on a road or other land – that appears to have broken down or been permitted to remain at rest in such a position or condition that it appears to the constable to have been abandoned without lawful authority.